FLIP

MENTAL TELEPATHY

Thomas Wayne Colby

THE INTERNAL HUMAN MIND KNOWS NO BOUNDARIES BUT

LOGIC

Table of Contents

Alphabetical Table of Contents

INTRODUCTION

All the mental telepathy described in this book or manual if you prefer, is the absolute truth unless noted as theory. The theories are my best guess as the authority of Flip Techniques at the time of this writing.

The name **"Flip"** here is just a popular and convenient nickname for telepathy. The reason I consider myself the authority on these subjects I describe is that I am the first one to write on these subjects. In addition I most certainly am the only one to write in this depth on these particular subjects. I am the first one in the history of mankind to practice Sound Telepathy, Foot Talking, Pure, and Image Mental Telepathy. I am the Inventor, Writer, and Teacher of True Mental Telepathy. There are no exaggerations or lies to trick people into buying or reading this book. The truth is so fantastic and novel that false fabrications are not needed to convince people of this new reality.

Telepathy was considered impossible before the writing of this book. This book is based on complete truth as its foundation or we would not have made it this far with these newly created realities. Telepathy or its nickname "Flip" seeks out the truth in the universe. Thought transference is one of the small trap doors of the human mind that leads into new universes' of infinite dimensions opening a multitude of resource doors inside these dimensions and making available new resources for the internal mind's concept formations and telepathy thought and image transmissions.

The Flip is a true form of Extra Sensory Perception that has expanded our communication senses. This Telepathy is for real and you will see this for yourself as you practice these basic skills in this book.

The Flip is growing stronger and changing daily at a terrific pace. Please remain flexible when you read this book's material. Although there is no misleading information in this book, the mental telepathy may take a different direction for you. If you see a different solution to achieve telepathy do not hesitate to follow it, provided it does not strain or hurt your mind. This mental telepathy is going to change as more people plug into it and begin to practice it. Some of the telepathy exercises seem silly but are normal daily occurrences in the course of everyday life that make them an easy way to learn and progress with telepathy. Before the writing of this book, all we had to go on were a few fuzzy clues but with the writing of this book we now have a true solid foundation to build telepathy with. This book is solid throughout with no exaggerations to throw you off. At first I thought Flip would most benefit handicapped people and then it went on to encompass all types of people of the world.

Telepathy is pure psychic intelligence; there is no physical human form.

In this book the terms Telepathy, Flip, Mind transference, Mind Meld, ESP, Thought Transference, Synchronized Psychic Energy with thought, and Mental Telepathy are used interchangeable in sentence to prevent redundancy. The **Telepathy is hard to explain clearly where it originates from** so a lot of telepathy words have been used in a sentence interchangeably to explain the origin of the telepathy communication transmissions.

I write the truth about mental telepathy, but I also leave some vague clues in my book that may be expanded by others leading to more advances in the mental telepathy field. This is the true beginning for telepathy and everything at this time is not totally clear, and you the reader in time might have things that you will add to the mind transference fundamentals.

In this book the word ***Conscience*** **means a morally encoded living long term memory** of all humans on earth that may be brought forward into the conscious and compared to your current operating concept presently in your conscious focus for moral correctness.

All this comparing is done in the ***Conscious*** **that is the area for all temporary**

construction and awareness of concepts imagined and also inputted information from the physical sense stimulus coming into the conscious from the outside environment. **Conscious memory remembers *physical input* for approximately 3 to 5 seconds**.

In addition **your conscious is able to view other peoples' consciouses by first entering a 3rd agreed working area called the *universal mind*** in this book. Likewise thought construction and telepathy viewing all take place from all participating minds in this agreed 3rd working area that is entered by way of the synchronization of conscious thought for a second time by two or more people that automatically enters this particular thought into the universal mind and this is called ***summation telepathy.***

Collective Moral Conscience is referred to in this book simply as the World Conscience, which is a living long term memory that is kept running by the interchanging morals of living minds possessed by current majority thinking.

The ***Collective Conscious*** is the awareness of present actual time concepts achieved by ***Summation Telepathy*** with other people and the name summation telepathy may be used interchangeably with collective conscious.

The **World Conscience**, **Collective Conscious** (or **Summation Telepathy),** are all found in the **Universal Mind** that runs telepathy by the synchronizing of two or more minds. The planet earth has billions of physical brains that plug into one unit called the ***Universal Mind*** that also has a chapter in this book along with all the above mentioned terms.

The words ***pre-cognitive*** and ***pre-conscious*** mean the same thing and are both used interchangeable and are found in the **glossary of terms at the end of this book that contains a few key word definitions for clarification of terms in this book. All bold words with italics have a definition in the glossary at the end of this book.**

Confusion: There is nothing in the writing of this book that is not totally simple. Some confusion will of course result from the readings. If you find yourself confused just backtrack and reread. All explanations are very simple but some confusion will result as you assemble multiple simple ***logic blocks***.

I the author Thomas Wayne Colby apologize to any man, woman or any other handicapped person offended by the wording in this book. It is not possible in the sentence structure to both explain telepathy thoroughly and also sugar coat everything as well. Thank You for Your Understanding.

Note to all the Skeptics of the world. I myself am one of the world's greatest skeptics and I do believe that is one of the reasons I was chosen for the writing of this telepathy. However it is my common sense duty as a Human Being to report the truth whatever the opinion. So I present you the truth of telepathy for your praise or scoff.

If you have any comments or questions I will try to answer them all. Please send them to:

tomwcolby@hotmail.com or colbytom@gmail.com

Cautions

What we are doing here in this book with telepathy has never been done before on planet earth. Therefore our pre-formed concepts of our past normal reality will cause us adults not to totally accept this new telepathy; for all we have ever known in this life makes mental telepathy seem impossible. With the writing of this book we begin to reshape our life's reality, but with the Flip going against everything we know as factual reality it will be very hard not to be skeptical of the truth of thought transference from time to time.

This thought transference practice will probably not drastically change an adult person's reality who encounters telepathy late in life; rather it will be a fragile and ephemeral addendum to an adult person's reality. Our generation of adults in society will begin to practice telepathy a little here and there over the course of our lifetimes viewing this Flip stuff simply as a fun fad. However the more people practicing telepathy and doing the impossible the more over time it will become more increasing real and popular.

Young children will view telepathy in a more encompassing and concrete way. The children exposed to telepathy at a young age will think that mental telepathy is a normal part of their everyday normal reality. As the child matures into an adult while at the same time practicing Flip techniques in the course of everyday life they will mold thought transference into their everyday reality making it a given, that has always been possible for the child throughout their entire life. It will be these children of the world that will take mental telepathy to new heights because of the amount of time practiced and their reality view of Flip.

One day you convince yourself the Flip is real and a helpful tool for mankind and the very next day you wake up with doubts about something that is new and seems impossible for the human mind. This telepathy will never be concrete in a person's mind if they started practicing Flip in their adult life without knowing it as a child. Our adult mind has many years of an established set of normal parameters that form our factual reality. Do not get frustrated with doubt concerning telepathy for even I the author find it hard to believe in this mind transference stuff totally on a daily basis.

I have come to realize the ironic truth that over the course of my lifetime the man that invented true mental telepathy will never truly believe in this new mental telepathy totally because I encountered it late in my adult life, 42. My adult mind and yours are too fickle and ephemeral in taking on new realities. Anxiety will result from our minds telling us that this telepathy has always been considered impossible by the masses before the writing of this book. The human mind resists changing its reality much the same way as a new heart recipient tries to reject its foreign new heart.

Our adult minds along with young children's minds will need constant validations or proof by other people repeating back to us vocally what our telepathy is attempting to project. To be on the safe side young children that are pre-schoolers should be validated every other word at this very young age. Adult mind's probably only need vocal verification of what is being said with your telepathy once a month. What is truly safe from a pre-schooler's every other word telepathy validation to once a month verification for adults I honestly cannot tell you. Thus care must be taken not to undermine a person's sense of reality by fooling with the impossible for too long a time without a vocal repetition from someone else verifying vocally what you intended to push out of your mind with telepathy transmission.

I have noticed that a lot of ***paranoid schizophrenics*** are not in the least bit afraid of mental telepathy rather they seem to enjoy it as much as the next person; if not more. **When I first noticed that paranoid schizophrenics were not afraid of mental telepathy I was very surprised because in the beginning I thought that Flip would hurt their mind and they would "freak out"**. So, on the contrary Flip is loved by mentally handicapped people and is very beneficial to them.

Usually I have noticed with myself that if my mind becomes over stimulated with telepathy it begins to shut it out automatically. A short nap always works for me if my mind is over stimulated, 10 to 20 minutes. I lot of times late in the evening telepathy begins to be too much for me and I shut it down going into the evening say 6 or 7 p.m.

If you continue to experience mental discomfort from mental telepathy I suggest you just abandon it totally; it is not that important in life if it promotes mental pain.

This book is to make people aware of what goes on in the world around them with thought transference communication. Being aware of telepathy makes a person capable of adjusting to it and possibly simply to recognize and ignore it. Telepathy is by no means a requirement in a person's life at this beginning stage of its development. As the author and creator of Flip I enjoy eye-to-eye contact talking and could live without telepathy communication in my life very easily. The Flip does have potential as a communication tool for mankind and we will now go forward with its discussion.

Psychic Energy and Physical Energies

Psychic Energy in this book Flip refers to energy that is not able to be defined by physical laws yet this different type of energy exists and is not dependent on physical energies to function nor is it bound to physical law limitations in its behavior. All normal thoughts in a person's physical human conscious are composed of this psychic energy, which is the "***container***" for holding all thought.

Normal physical human bio-chemical thinking with its sodium, potassium, and chloride ions all react back and forth in the cellular neurons inside the physical brain giving electrical power that fires among billions of interconnecting neurons that science states occurs in milliseconds. **This bio-chemical electrical power is synchronized with a normal thought that is held in a container or field of psychic energy resulting in the normal thought being captured in the conscious.** The human mind's physical bio-chemical energy synchronizes this container of psychic energy containing a thought allowing for the perception and holding of the thought in the human conscious. By holding this particular chosen psychic thought in your conscious for a short time by this bio-chemical electricity, construction and examination of the thought can occur.

However normal bio-chemical synchronized containers of psychic thought inside the human mind are not capable to be transmitted as telepathic thought to other conscious minds when first learning telepathy without an ***auxiliary helper***. A human's conscious container of captured psychic thought is not shared by other people until it is sent to an agreed physical synchronized point (auxiliary helper) that is outside the conscious. Two or more people are capable of sharing a conscious thought when it is synchronized with a physical auxiliary helper with rhythm first, this physical rhythm (auxiliary helper) is shared by all people due to the fact it is a given of physical law shared by all humans.

Agreed physical world auxiliary helpers such as sound, light, vibrations, body motion, contact touching, and the human heartbeat are first needed as the physical sequence that synchronizes the human mind's psychic packets of conscious thought. The combination of psychic packets of conscious thought with an auxiliary helper provides a vehicle to take all telepathic thought into the universal mind for summation telepathy viewing by others. When a container of psychic thought from the human conscious is synchronized for a second time with an auxiliary helper from the physical world the thought instantly enters the universal mind and is available for telepathic summation viewing by all people.

The 3rd work area in this book is referred to as the ***Universal Mind*** and has a small descriptive chapter of its own. This 3rd workplace may be called a higher dimensional level of conscious but this telepathy is brand new and for now the nomenclature will be universal mind for clarity.

An agreed shared physical synchronization point may be sound, vibration or light; the agreement part here is the knowledge by two or more people that these physical facts exist and are agreed on by these people. Once inside the universal mind the thought is available for the entire universe to view by physical proximity or by conscious selection and this shared viewing I assign the name of ***summation telepathy*.**

The universal mind further synchronizes all thoughts that enter it and in time a person may master (through facilitation) entering the dimension of the universal mind without the need for physical auxiliary helpers using the psychic thought alone. After a few months to a few years of practicing telepathy the human conscious gains the ability to synchronize psychic containers of captured conscious thought for a 2nd time for telepathic transmission without using outside physical synchronization points. This telepathy performed with the absence of auxiliary helpers is called "**Pure**" thought telepathy. Internal **Pure** telepathy synchronization automatically enters the universal mind but is difficult and must be learned over time. Although **Pure** along with **Image Flip** are more difficult techniques of telepathy an amateur when familiar with telepathy concepts will on occasion perform these difficult techniques well. **Image Flip** is the highest level of telepathy above **Pure** and also has a chapter in this book.

Physical telepathic synchronization points are needed in the beginning phases of telepathy and when they have been agreed on by millions of people this makes them a given that cannot be refused by a human conscious when a telepathic thought is attached with rhythm such as sight and sound. Agreed also means that the synchronization points are shared by all people of the world particularly those within 100 meters radius of the synchronization point. These auxiliary helpers have a pushed out thought from the originator's conscious attached to them with synchronized precision or rhythm when using sound, light, or vibration.

Telepathy concepts are sent as a psychic energy thought from the human conscious to a physical synchronization point outside the conscious, which then snaps it into the universal mind or it enters directly without auxiliary helpers into the universal mind enabling the thought to be viewed by 2 to an infinity number of people inside the universal mind.

A Telepathy concept is formed, transmitted, and received as noted in the following:

Transmission of a Telepathic Thought

1 - Originator of a telepathic thought captures and holds a normal thought by physical bio-chemical energy, which is presently synchronizing a normal conscious thought contained in a field of psychic energy in his or her conscious.

2 - Originator then synchronizes this captured conscious thought for a second time by "pushing it" to an outside physical agreed synchronization point such as sound, light, touching, or vibration that now combines with this particular conscious thought outside the conscious making this thought available to be viewed by two or more people. **Agreed physical world synchronization points** or **auxiliary helpers** are simple physical senses that teach telepathy synchronization in the outside world allowing for the entering into the universal mind or 3rd work area and also give confidence in the reality of telepathy when sensed as physical and tangible. In the beginning the physical sense world is easier to understand in the use of synchronization for telepathy. Pure telepathy may bypass the physical world when learned and go directly into the universal mind.

3 - After synchronizing this particular psychic telepathic thought in the physical world with an auxiliary helper it automatically snaps instantly into the universal mind. **Once inside the universal mind all consciouses in the immediate area (approximately 100 meters) will view the thought;** in addition with proper location and familiarity the telepathy thought is able to transverse the entire universe and back instantly.

CHARACTERISTICS OF PSYCHIC ENERGY

1 - Psychic energy is a container that holds all thoughts of the universe.

2 - Psychic energy is a vehicle for transportation of thought.

3 - Psychic energy may copy a thought exactly and completely.

4 - Psychic energy pieces concepts together from multiple sources other than the originator of the thought (summation telepathy).

5 - Psychic energy from others illuminates low energy concepts in conscious and pre-conscious

so they may be recognized by the consciouses of both the originator of the telepathy concept and the other person viewing it.

6 - Psychic energy sends conscious thought transmissions out to an infinite distance

once inside the universal mind capable of being received by infinite number of human minds.

7 - Psychic energy is able to be synchronized with normal human bio-chemical energy.

8- Psychic energy is also able to be synchronized with physical world ***auxiliary helpers*** outside the conscious for transmission of telepathy.

9 - Psychic energy is able to link an infinite number of consciouses together for thought process sharing that I call ***telepathy summation***.

10 - Psychic energy is able to be synchronized internally in the conscious mind for a second time making telepathy possible without the use of auxiliary helpers and this automatically puts it into the universal mind and this is called **Pure** telepathy.

11 - Telepathy transverses the entire universe and back again in less than .1 of a second putting the speed of telepathy over 20 billion light years in .1 of a second; which the Chandler Radio Telescope has measured for us.

By reverse engineering we are able to say that **psychic energy is also able to link an infinite number of physical neural junction boxes together inside the human physical mind.**

This linking together of physical neural junction boxes by psychic energy will aid with the rerouting and repairing of damaged human physical brain systems. Thought packets residing in a psychic energy container that are now taking an alternate route via telepathy synchronization will help to repair the nervous system line and move the thought along to the conscious restoring normal thought processes again.

FLIP

(Telepathy)

Bio-chemical electrical processes of the human physical brain synchronize and capture all conscious thoughts, which are normally contained in a field of psychic energy. Thoughts synchronized by bio-chemical electricity are captured and held in the conscious gallery for time allowing for the further examination and construction of a thought.

Telepathy uses Psychic Energy Packets of conscious thought that are synchronized for a second time by other means than bio-chemical energy. Psychic thought transmission is a given as psychic energy is in abundance in the universe and is free for the taking. The problem telepathy has with this abundance of free psychic energy containing packets of conscious thought is the necessity to first send the conscious thought to an agreed 3rd synchronization point. This sending of a conscious thought to a distinct area other than the originator's conscious for synchronization enables the originator's conscious concept to be viewed in another person's conscious via this 3rd area; the originator and receiver being the 1st and 2nd points involved.

In order for a particular conscious thought to become telepathic it must first be sent from the sender's conscious mind to this 3rd work area, which I have named the ***universal mind*** in my book. Once the thought enters the universal mind it is available for viewing by all intelligence life in the universe; generally the concept is transmitted out to 1000 meters, more commonly in everyday life telepathy transmission is perceived in a 100 meter radius of the originator of a telepathic thought.

Agreed physical world auxiliary helpers such as sound, light, vibrations, body motion, contact touching, and the human heartbeat are first needed as the physical world synchronized vehicles for gaining access into the universal mind by synchronizing the conscious's psychic packets of thought for a 2nd time. **The combination of psychic packets of conscious thought and the secondary synchronization by auxiliary helpers provides a vehicle to take all telepathic thought into the universal mind for summation telepathy viewing by others.**

A telepathic thought may also be sent to the universal mind directly without the aid of auxiliary helpers and this is an advanced form of secondary synchronization telepathy called Pure, which has a chapter of its own in this book. Pure telepathy takes a little longer to learn requiring the beginner to first use the much easier physical sense auxiliary helpers for secondary sychronization, which also are sensed to the human mind easier as a real event.

In past history many types of auxiliary helpers were in existence that served only to build a person's confidence enabling them to think that they could perform different types of telepathy or extra sensory perception. Things such as quartz rocks, pyramids, Ouija boards, unsynchronized bells and many other sounds not synchronized along with countless other lucky charms were used to give confidence to mankind in the past. These physical objects gave confidence to psychic individuals to pull off random events of psychic thought transmission but all of these devices failed to synchronize the thought for a second time in the conscious resulting in failure to enter the universal mind for telepathic viewing by other people. At best unsynchronized telepathy is just weak mental drift that is very hazy and unclear telepathy and totally random in its transmission and reception.

Now in the 21st century we look to proven physical auxiliary helpers with conscious synchronization for constructing telepathy such as the techniques described in this book. It is generally necessary at first to use an auxiliary helper for learning secondary thought synchronization such as described in the following.

First you form a word in your conscious mind that you wish to push out to

others as thought transference. Concentrating on this word inside your mind, you now break the word into syllables. Next you imagine pushing the word out of your internal conscious mind into the precise matching beat of a sound, flash of light; or vibration with one synchronized syllable of word per beat of sound and also one syllable of word into a single flash of a strobe light.

Another popular agreed synchronization point for psychic energy transfer enabling telepathy observance of thought is the striking point of the human body in motion such as a footstep coming into contact with the ground. As your foot touches the ground you push out from your mind one syllable of word into each step as it contacts the ground. Foot talking has a following chapter of its own as well as Sound Flip and Motion Flip.

The nice thing about basic telepathy skills is that they can be performed with just a pair of hands clapping or the feet walking as described in sound Flip and foot talking sections.

At times a person sending the telepathy transmission does not have a complete understanding of the concept they are sending or the sound volume being sent is weak. In either case of incompleteness the mind of the receiver makes instant adjustments automatically without his or her conscious selection by matching the inputted telepathy concept and adding pieces from their memories along with the amplification of the original sender's Flip transmission sound.

A third working area or mind is created where pieces of the concept from both minds and possibly more than these original two minds assemble a telepathy concept until it becomes more recognizable than the original capabilities of the two separate minds. At times neither of the individuals involved in telepathy summation will possess the total knowledge for completing the concept for total recognition in their conscious minds. As the two minds hook together in ***summation telepathy*** they enrich the concept more through this third workplace created between two or more minds. These two people construct by summation telepathy and also borrow from other pertinent minds of the universe generally in close proximity. In addition telepathy opens various dimensional doors making available different resources all inside the internal human mind that all become available to enrich the original concept. Common working distance for the telepathy is usually in the proximity of 100 meters, easily encompassing 500 meters at times.

Telepathy concept transmissions take all aware conscious minds *familiar* and also those simply in close *proximity* into this universal mind's dimension automatically by secondary synchronization of a particular thought. All minds being in thought synchronization going into the universal mind at an exact moment in time enables everyone involved to take full advantage of all these construction resources in this universal area for enhancing all thoughts. All this telepathy concept construction takes place instantly inside the universal mind and is called summation telepathy. The word summation here meaning two or more minds working together to solve a problem by assembling pieces possessed by all minds involved in the telepathy summation for a more clearer and recognizable concept.

In essence all telepathy that involves two or more minds is also automatically summation telepathy.

This synchronization of thought opens the doors to an infinite number of dimensions of telepathy inside the human mind via the universal mind. These inner dimensions of the mind may be given various names as we are not sure what they really are at this time. I do not know if these dimensions are black holes, infinite parallel universes, super stars, or possible just **dimensional levels of intelligent thought**. These inner dimensions of the mind have doors or levels that are open with different types of psychic energy mind control. These dimensional doors inside the mind normally refuse to be opened in the higher dimensional levels without first learning to pass through the lower level dimensions; appearing to be chronological occurring with depth.

It is possible to aim telepathy at a single individual in a crowd of a hundred thousand people attending a football game in a stadium. This individual who you have singled out of the crowd to communicate telepathy with knows that he or she is the sole aim of your communication. In addition to the intended sole recipient hearing or seeing the concept of thought transference sent by me or you, all one hundred thousand people in the stadium crowd will also be capable hearing or seeing the image thought transference transmission. The crowd of 100,000 people will also recognize the target individual as the sole intended receptor of the Flip even though everybody in the crowd overhears all the telepathy communication. I could also do a general broadcast to the whole crowd of 100,000 people simultaneously using the crowd's roar noise with no particular individual as the target of the mental telepathy transmission.

In addition I could also create the projected image illusion of a circle around a person's head in the crowd of one hundred thousand people. This type of telepathy image projection will also single the person out in the crowd and is another form of making sure the person knows that the mind transference was intended for them. All people in the crowd although meant for one person in particular can view all these types of mental telepathy projections as they occur. **A person can also simply feel the focused energy by itself of telepathy upon them singling them out without image projection or sound added.** Image projection has its own chapter in this book and is the highest level of Flip.

This is a peculiarity of telepathy as we now begin to develop it; the fact that all mind transference is fed into the ***universal mind*** for observation by all people. Good or bad I do not know, but everyone no matter who it was intended for can always view or hear the telepathy generally in a 500 meter radius of the transmitter if intense, 100 meters for common everyday telepathy.

Another example would be a crowded cafeteria as you practice mind transference intended for a single individual. Although intended for only one person in the crowded cafeteria everyone will over hear all telepathy conversation said. Definitely not private communication at present but I am sure in the near future people will figure a way to more privatize personal conversations of telepathy.

In the future all thoughts will be able to be scrutinized by the people of the world by telepathy through the universal mind. Now is not a bad time to begin to align your childrens' minds towards more ethical thoughts because as we move into the future these thoughts will be scrutinized more and therefore judged.

It is also possible to Flip two thoughts at once or pretty damn close to simultaneous. The second thought is weaker in nature in comparison to the primary thought but it is recognized as another separate thought only quieter.

Well memorized phrases from hit songs, television theme songs, or famous actors' voices are easily recognized when projected with mind transference because of their familiarity. Popular songs in big city rush hour traffic are a lot of fun to Flip out into the mass of vehicles. The large number of vehicles involved in the daily commute of city workers supplies the **auxiliary sound** needed for synchronization of sound telepathy that is discussed in more detail in one of the following chapters titled Sound Flip.

Many people are eager to respond to your Flip in rush hour traffic making this a favorite place to practice sound telepathy. In moving vehicles and especially when traffic is heavy, everyone is anonymous and less hesitant about Flipping and joining in to respond to mental telepathy. **Anonymity much like drunkenness dis-inhibits people into doing things they normally would not do in public** and with a lot of people in moving cars no one really knows who initiates the Flip.

When done with anonymous partners such as the scenario of fast moving cars in rush hour traffic or in the dark of night Flip telepathy accentuates the aspect of no human form involving only the communication of thoughts. You really do not know the way a person looks or their ethnic background when you are doing a casual sound Flip in rush hour traffic or in the dark of night. **This aspect about mental telepathy by casual communication in large crowds without the observation of the speaking individuals begins to make a person understand prejudice in the physical human form.**

You will never ever understand why certain looking individuals have been stereotyped by your mind after sound Flipping in rush hour traffic or nighttime driving. It is very easy to love someone's thoughts without the prejudice of body form such as color, race, or beauty causing one to judge their thoughts.

There is no way in an anonymous Flip that you can pick up a person's race or primary language group, however accents can be easily added if desired. A person may Flip a word that he or she does not comprehend the meaning of as long as they have a grasp as to what the word should sound like. Therefore, if a person understands somewhat the pronunciation of the word they can pass themselves off as the correct nationality of the intended Flip when anonymous by being unseen.

People can Flip any sound or foreign word they wish and the sounds of it will be perceived but perhaps not the meaning of the word. Often times the response will be to repeat the Flipped word or sound they heard and usually this is followed by the phrase, "Huh! What does that word mean"? They will hear the exact phonics of the word or sound you intended to Flip; even though the person listening is not familiar with the word from this language they usually will repeat it back vocally correct. I have Flipped Chinese words and Native American words familiar to practically no one in the vicinity and gotten total reception of the intended telepathy sounds with voice feedback.

As you get better with Flip you will able to add emotion to your Flips. **Everybody recognizes emotion in Flips but this is perceived on a more varied degree not**

like ordinary word Sound Flipping that everybody picks up perfectly if in close proximity of 500 meters. Emotions will also be discussed again in a later chapter in this book.

Flip leads to sharpened senses increasing in sensitivity as the time practiced increases, becoming more aware of noise and vibration occurring around you in the world. **Flip also seems to open more dimensional doors in the mind for information that provide additional resources for problem solving.** Telepathy may be able to help a person's mind with one bad eye to learn to see through both eyes as the one good eye does.

I worked in California and the adjoining western states for two years as a truck driver. In those two years I taught or spread Flip throughout the Western United States working with other truck drivers along with the cars as I traveled the highways. Flipping with your vehicle in traffic on the West Coast has become an acceptable and everyday practice in that part of the country in the United States. This telepathy all started to really grow in the second half of 1998. This thought transference stuff is still new in most places of the United States and the rest of the world for that matter but in time telepathy will grow to be an awesome part of our life well into the future.

At first, I thought this "Flipping" would help stroke patients, accident victims, or handicapped people with speech problems. Some people have a difficult time speaking in this world for whatever the reason and I thought that mental telepathy could help. In the very beginning I thought that maybe crumbling papers or scratching a rough surface (like sandpaper) would enable these people to conveniently communicate if their vocals were not able to function due to mental or physical damage.

Physics of Telepathy - I have not tried to explain the physics of Flip; for one thing I would have to do a lot of research and we would still only be making wild guesses at this point. There is not enough physical energy in the physical brain to do mental telepathy according to physics so we run into problems explaining telepathy communication physics right from the start. **For now it is best to call telepathy a given; the same as gravity**. We know that when two or more masses come together gravity occurs that really is not explained just said to be a given. The same holds true for mental telepathy; **when two or more minds come together there is thought transference occurring and summating out to infinite distances and this is a given.**

Speed of Telepathy Theory - Does the speed of Flip increase the deeper it runs in the mind or is the time dimension warped a bit inside the human mind? The human mind must create a dimension with no time that telepathy may take advantage of or simply the mind in certain areas is ignorant of time and pays no attention to it as it must be not needed in some dimensions of the human internal mind. Does summation group telepathy increase this speed of thought even more inside the internal human mind, as the more speed gained the less time consumed?

Thought transference goes against the laws of physics because the recognition of the telepathy and the response time is lacking and unaccounted for in physical time measurement of mind transference concepts. Pure Flip is transmitted, received, and repeated back vocally by the receiver all simultaneously. On some occasions pure Flip seems to be sent back with vocal recognition before it is completely transmitted from the originator's mind creating some kind of time gain here. A few people are so quick at repeating thoughts vocally back to me I barely know I thought them.

If two people were capable of "Pure" thought transference the speed of the telepathy would be fantastic, as the minds would not slow down while they pause for a breath of air as in speaking. People are unaware that their minds are trained to take brief pauses for a breath of air, which slows talking and thinking down quite a bit.

Flip telepathy is going to travel to farthest corner of the universe and back again in less than a tenth of a second(.1 second), which the Chandler Radio Telescope tells us is over ten billion light years away; completing this total distance of 20 billion light years in less than a tenth of a second. In the inner dimensions of the human mind any concept is possible as long as it has logical reasoning as its basis; and the idea need not obey any physical law of the universe when inside the internal mind's dimensions.

Even though all the people in the world cannot transmit the higher forms of telepathy, everybody in the world can receive all forms of telepathy perfectly the first time. This makes us conclude that Flip is an innate normal form of communication for the human mind taking a little more time to learn the Pure Telepathy ***transmission*** process. The Flip is pre-programmed for reception at birth, this telepathy coming on strong when normal language skills begin. It is also very probable that synchronization of thought for telepathy can occur to the fetus inside the womb of their mother as it develops.

Telepathy Characteristics

1- Increased Sensory Perception, amplification, and clarification of all incoming physical senses including emotions.

2- Thought Transmission.

3- Image Projection.

4- Thought Sharing and Sense Sharing normally called **summation telepathy** in this book, which amplifies the original concept and adds pieces for completeness.

5- ILLUSION of Sensory Perception or Artificial Creation of physical sense from memory.

6- Thought Slowing, Blocking, and Interference.

7- Thought Control and Repelling of Unwanted Thoughts in the conscious zone.

8- Holding Thoughts in the Conscious Focus of Another.

9- Thought Construction.

10- Transparency of Conscious Thought and Images to all People of the World.

11- Agreement of Thought or Disagreement of Thought (Judgment). When your concept is viewed by others with telepathy other people let you know if the thought is in harmony giving reinforcement of this particular thought that gives a good feeling. When in disagreement with others telepathy will help to morally correct bad concepts and give a feeling of incorrectness or sometimes chastisement enforcing morals.

12- Meditation Solo or in Summation.

13- Telepathy Utilizes Psychic Energy Not Physical Energy.

14- Mental Telepathy will now begin to be a new School of Psychology.

15- Telepathy opens dimensional doors to an infinite number of new dimensions inside the human internal mind for adding new resources for problem solving and building new concepts.

16- A route for venting Stress.

17- Rerouting thought through broken or damaged neural pathways by psychic energy.

18- Time Gain.

19- Premonitions or simply said predicting future events.

20- Synchronization of conscious thought with sound telepathy.

21- Dream suggestion

22- Addicting qualities and hard to quit due to the human mind demanding communication and socialization as a daily function.

Social Theory of Learning - Whenever you teach a large group of people or community mental telepathy, (say a hundred or more) it seems like the next new group of people in another city or state even though they are not familiar with mental telepathy are already facilitated for Flip. **Even though this new group of people**

has never experienced Flip before they will now perform the telepathy skills as well as the last experienced group and quite often a little better almost immediately. This prior group that had practiced telepathy skills has facilitated the mainframe computer for telepathy or the ***universal mind*** for the following group in time. Note: After 10 years of practicing telepathy in numerous cities in USA, France, Germany, India, Bangladesh, Cambodia, Mexico, Costa Rica, Nicaragua, and Panama, this Social Theory is now a fact but I will leave it here as theory so it serves as an example how telepathy theory hardens over time. This Social Theory of learning is hard Fact at present but in 1998 when it was first written it was a simple "WILD" Theory.

Speed of light telepathy versus speed of sound telepathy. This is a unique experience that uses auxiliary helpers but I think it belongs here.

A crew of 4 men were working on a railroad track driving spikes against the steel rails with a large sledge hammer about 250 meters down the railroad track from my observation point. I noticed the impact of the sledgehammer as it came into contact with the railroad spike and I Flipped this image synchronization point. After a moment following the sight of the hammer strike came the sound of the strike and I then Flipped a syllable of word with the sound of the hammer. So I was able to differentiate between light and sound because the sound was slower than light and I synchronized both with Flip projection.

Some final notes on Flip: **Telepathy should only be done live and in person, and not from any recorded medium. Confusion will result if telepathy reception is attempted from movies or television.** The people you observe appearing on the television are not in synchronization due to pre-recording and also live broadcasts sometimes contain a time delay of 5-10 seconds for censorship of these live broadcasts. In addition the guy the down the street or across town, possible even around the world could be using the sounds of the television for their own sound telepathy overriding the actors' telepathy on the television or your telepathy.

A person should take good care of their mental health because people in their eighties seem to Flip a little better than most people even though they are old.

Universal Mind

In the universal mind any number of physical brains can hook themselves into this single mind of the universe by first telepathy synchronizing their conscious thoughts. **When practicing Flip all humans in the universe transmit to this single mind and receive from this same single mind of the universe.** So there are an infinite number of physical brains existing in the universe but in reality only one mind in the universe that we as human physical brains interconnect to for telepathy. I give this dimension of telepathy the name ***universal mind***. This telepathy hook up with the universal mind allows for simultaneous thought transmissions and receptions throughout the universe and may also allow thoughts to go back and forth through time, if only for a few seconds. In addition the universal mind helps to add parts to a concept by building this concept or making it more clear in its detail this done by searching other resources made available through telepathy.

The more people practicing mental telepathy, the more people will be in synchronization with the universal mind,which makes available a multitude of inner mind resource dimensions that contain higher intelligence. Along with the availability of higher intelligence resources will be a domineering ethical conscience that I call the ***World Conscience*** in this book, all contained inside the universal mind.

Really this World Conscience should be called the Universal Social Conscience or Universal Moral Conscience as the Flip is designed to travel through the entire universe and return instantly. This wording will lead to confusion with too many universal words here so we will go with the word "World" for differentiation of terms between the two concepts of universal mind and universal social conscience.

This is why in time people should practice ethics in mental telepathy and not download too much negative information into the mainframe (universal mind). In theory the universal mind should attack instantly and destroy or dismantle all illogical thoughts that enter it, possible by repelling or pushing them back into the pre-conscious trash area. Evil thoughts are illogical and may not assemble with the other basic principle logic blocks as they are foreign and not in harmony with logical majority thinking. As more people learn telepathy, more power will be contained inside the universal mind to do good things by moral pressure.

As a person practices mental telepathy more and more over time the mental telepathy becomes increasingly easy to slip into as an automatic conscious process. Going into the near future all of a person's conscious thought will enter the universal mind for examination and scrutinization by ***conscious transparency***, which is the simple viewing of all conscious thought discussed later in the book in the chapter of Telepathic Examination of others thought and Transparency. Again, conscious transparency and all telepathy concepts in general will normally be occurring in a 100 meter radius but may easily extend out to 1000 meters with more conscious effort. If addressed correctly by familiarity and known location telepathy concepts will be able travel the entire universe.

The universal mind should be weighted towards what the majority of people on earth think about normalcy and since mental telepathy is a higher form of thinking a more ethical conscience should be entered here as this is only logical. **A person should begin to feel the weight of this universal social conscience or world conscience viewing them.** In time this world conscience should begin to overpower unethical thoughts and actions through the influence and if necessary the coercing of peoples' mind that will help a person to choose a more correct life.

The universal mind is an area that contains infinite doors to other levels of intelligent resource dimensions making the universal mind Infinite.

The universal mind contains an infinite number of dimensional doors that open to resources of intelligence but these doors are chronological levels that have to be built to and order must generally be maintained to reach and have access to a particular dimensional door.

The universal mind is also able to be viewed by all physical brains in the universe at the same time with telepathy; and the **World Conscience is a continuing living Long Term Memory inside the Universal mind** for comparing moral and logical correct thoughts to the majority's thinking for logic and morals.

Goals of the Universal Mind

1- Synchronization of Telepathy Thought

2- Summation of Telepathy Thought (Hooking an infinite number of minds together for a common goal)

3- Communication of Thought

4- Communication of Senses, sound, sight, touch, emotion, taste, and smell.

5- Keys to Doors of various internal mind Thinking Dimensions containing added intelligence resources.

6- Clarity of Thought Increases along with amplification.

7- Harmony of Thought that gives "Good Feeling" of correctness.

8- Moral Pressure resulting in policing the conscious along with correct thinking conscious suggestions.

9- Control of Violent Thought

10- Self-Activation

11- Quietness

12- Soul communication

Sound Flip

When working with sound Flip a person in the beginning stages has to be in control of the sound producing device thereby manipulating the sound a bit. Later in this book we will discuss other ways of sound telepathy, but in the beginning everyone should start out by manipulating the sound device manually. Hand clapping is one of the simplest forms of sound Flip with only the human body needed. Note: Sound is a physical world ***auxiliary helper*** for synchronization and sometimes simply supplies confidence for performing telepathy.

Other techniques of sound Flip require controlling the rhythmic beats of sound or regulating revolutions per minute of a motor. The rhythmic beat of a motor is easy to pick up and alter through very slight pressure on the throttles. Musical instruments such as a guitar, piano, or drum can be used for telepathy by controlling the sounds of the musical instrument as you play them with your hand or mouth for wind instruments. The beat of the music does not have to be a constant rhythm; it only has to produce sound. With the addition of Flip, live rock and roll music and live symphony performances will take on a different aspect with thoughts interwoven in the music.

To Sound Flip you start by breaking a word into syllables in your conscious mind and then match one syllable of word with one beat of a sound. You then push the word syllable out of your conscious mind into the beat of a sound; one syllable of word per one beat of sound. This matching of word syllables with sound beats is called ***synchronization***. If the push of the word syllable into the beat of music is not synchronized properly the word Flip will not be clear with the sound used. With just a little more concentration focused on the word-syllable synchronization with the sound beat these discrepancies or fuzziness of sound telepathy will clear up. The word synchronization used in this book refers to the timing of the attachment of the word syllable to the beat of sound.

So when first starting out with Flip you will need to break the word into syllables. Such as the following example "Good (one syllable) Morn-ing (two syllables). So the word Good=one beat of sound and Morning=two beats of sound. **Some words are clearer in your mind than others to Flip with so if you have difficulty with one word simply exchange it with another easier word that sounds clearer inside your mind that has the same meaning.** Sometimes the word in another language is spoken clearer inside your mind. In this example here the word "Good" in Good Morning is not the easiest word to Flip with as the word "Good" sounds a little fuzzy in the conscious but with practice it will become a little clearer in your mind to push out. On the other hand, "Buenos Dias" is very easy to do the first time with basically the same meaning.

Common sounds to work with are: traffic noise, motors, compressed air, musical instruments (notes and percussion). Skate boarders, and Rollerbladers really go all out for this stuff with the sound of their wheels sound Flipping words. Footsteps in stone gravel, footsteps in cold crunchy icy snow, snow skiing noise made while turning, kicking sport balls of all kinds and footsteps with hard soled shoes on a hard surface are also excellent sounds to Flip with. Walking on the beach with your feet wading through the beach surf producing splashing sounds is fun and easy to do with sound Flip.

Let us throw wind into this group of sounds for telepathy also. On a really windy day a person can manipulate his or her hat to produce sound telepathy Flipping words with a moderate to strong wind deflecting off their hat. Telepathy with wind sounds deflecting off your face, ears, or your hat are soothing and sometimes a little spooky sounding and a lot of fun to do.

To start off your day you may add motivating words to sound telepathy such as "*win this day*" as you are towel drying or combing your hair after your morning shower. I towel dry my hair after every shower while repeating the words "win this day" with the towel's sound and touch. This towel drying your hair and Flipping helps hold your focus and motivate you into having a nice productive day.

Children bouncing a rubber ball may Flip syllables of words or spell words one letter at a time such as c-a-t into the sound of the ball as it strikes the ground. **Bouncing a ball and inserting sound telepathy is very easy to do and a lot of fun for children.** This bouncing ball Flip is an excellent way for adults to instruct children in simple spelling of words or reciting A-B-C's while at play. Some young children are hyperactive and may benefit tremendously from doing this bouncing ball telepathy and spelling words or perhaps with foot talking telepathy spelling words. The sound of the rubber ball smacking on a hard surface makes this bouncing ball telepathy a little easier to transmit telepathy with than foot talking, which is discussed in the following chapter.

This bouncing ball sound telepathy spelling game is an example of **passive learning,** which children have no objection to practicing. When your child is forced to sit down and learn to read or spell words they object because they are forced against their will. Learning for the young child is a little painful as concentration is difficult for the young individual's mind whereas game playing is fun.

Driving a car produces all kinds of noises and vibrations to practice sound Flip with. Noise from the tire contact with the road surface, wind turbulence, motor revolutions, and the car's drive train all produce noise. The operator of an automobile is in control of the motor and therefore the speed of the auto regulating this speed of the vehicle by accelerator movements. The more velocity the vehicle has, the more noise is available for Flip. Even extremely light pressure on the throttle will make the necessary fluctuation in motor revolutions for talking with sound Flip. Just placing your foot or hand on the throttle or accelerator without movement is sometimes enough to provide the slight nuances of sound to Flip with from the motor and car's movement noise.

The louder the sound of your source the easier *telepathy synchronization* is going to be for the simple reason that the extra loudness is an increase in physical energy, which facilitates the synchronization of conscious thought into the universal mind. This extra loudness will require less hand pressure or foot movement on the throttles. For example a jet airplane is so loud that the pilot could easily Flip word syllables into the jet motor noise simply by leaning his little finger on the throttle stick without any movement at all. The jet motors put out tremendous energy that a person is able to take advantage of for sound Flip.

Solo Sound Flip - It is possible that a person may also use a radio headset along with a portable CD player that is playing a strong music beat, and using this beat to perform sound Flip **solo** without any other person hearing this sound auxiliary helper inside your headphones. This sounds impossible but ***physical auxiliary helpers*** actually are not needed to perform advanced telepathy; the secondary synchronization of conscious thought may be provided by the internal mind only and is called Pure Flip.

If a person wanted a little help in forming words in their mind for telepathy they could move their lips without speaking any vocal sounds (Lip Sync). I sometimes move my lips during Flip giving intensity and clarity to the Flip a bit. This of course alerts people watching you that you are the one who is doing the telepathy as they notice your lips moving. Therefore you can move your lips if you so desire, this however is not necessary for telepathy as this lip sync provides a helping device of sorts for forming clearer sounds inside your mind.

One of the more peculiar sounds to use for telepathy is running water that also happens to be one of the easiest sounds to Flip with by pushing words into the sound of the flowing water. A person may manipulate a water hose Flipping words with the sound of the splashing water very easily.

Large fountains or strong flowing water such as a fast moving river

sometimes have the capability of sounding holy if a *person chooses to listen for telepathy* from these sources of sound. As one listens to the sound of the flowing water meditating and adding telepathy synchronization to the noise of the water, vague voices will appear to come from the sound of the flowing water. These voices coming from the flowing water sound holy as if messages from God. I think that maybe a person's pre-conscious space debris thoughts (illogical junk) are coming forward into our conscious awareness through this water sound with the addition of ***telepathy listening***. All and all, strong flowing water sound is not a reliable interpretation device for listening for telepathy.

However a person may push their conscious thoughts into the strong flowing water just remember not to "listen" for vague voices coming from the water.

A person could easily believe that they are channeling with this water as if listening to dead people or people from other dimensions of the mind sending holy messages, but please do not let yourself fall for this catastrophe of jumbled thoughts. Water may easily be used for **transmitting** sound telepathy; just be aware that you should not listen for other weak thoughts in the sound of the water floating through haphazardly. If you try this listening around flowing water or fountains you will see what I am trying to point out to you. Just be aware if you are **meditating** around running water your mind can play tricks on you. I would not suggest too much of this running water "listening" because it is very difficult to control and you could make yourself sick.

You should also be aware not to listen for vague voices blowing in the wind. Always remember that pushing thoughts into noise with Flip transmission and listening to vague thoughts are two different techniques of telepathy.

In general vague sound Flip should not be listened for in blowing wind or flowing water as mental telepathy is a little more clearly sent and is not vague. Do not strain your mind to listen to flotsam and space debris of the universe that makes no sense, real telepathy comes clear. **Beware of things that can make you sick very easily by listening to sounds that are probably just your mind throwing bits and pieces away through imaginative daydreaming with Flip synchronization.**

Just a word of advice here about practicing telepathy with sound around loud machinery in the factory setting as it pertains to safety. Sound telepathy may be sometimes be considered dangerous around machinery due to distraction; but if the work environment is too loud to talk above, sound Flip may be safer than no communication at all and it is extremely easy to do around loud machinery. **The sound telepathy may serve as warning to prevent injury, as continual vocal warning can be tiring in the course of a day's work where as mental telepathy warnings are not tiring.** Sound Flip is a lot easier to perform constantly and is also a lot less offensive to the minds' of your co-workers and can improve worker safety around machinery. Safety is first around machinery and should not be taken for granite.

I would like to relate a cute story here on how sound Flip can be beneficial at times.

A dump truck was heading into an elementary school zone while school was in session but the truck driver was speeding way too fast with children around the school. I used sound Flip from the noises the truck was making, i.e. wind, diesel motor, bumping noises from the metal parts of the tailgate as it went too fast over a speed bump, to Flip the words "slow down or we'll call the police" in my mind without speaking but using the truck's sounds for Flip communication at a distance of 300 meters. The truck driver thought he was hearing an actual voice in the neighborhood voicing their disagreement and yelled back out his truck window, "sorry I'll slow down". The truck driver perceived the sound Flip as a normal voice in the neighborhood.

I had did sound Flip thousands of times prior to this trucker but this incident made me laugh and I always remember this one because it made a vivid impression in my mind that I had slowed a large vehicle down for safety with telepathy. **I would like to mention that this sound Flip from a distance of 300 meters cannot be accomplished right away and needs to be progressed to but in time it becomes easy to do.**

I would like to add a tidbit here for us to ponder. Is some normal speaking really a form of mental telepathy with sound? We all have encountered people that slur or use slang that is barely recognizable as human speech, could this really be in some part a form of mental telepathy with sound?

Sound Flip may help astronauts in space when the radio goes dead but possesses a static noise signal to transmit mental telepathy with sound and of course Flip will also work through any radio static here on planet earth. This radio static from space sounds extremely far out but it is simple to do as basic sound telepathy as you are in control of the radio.

Teaching sound Flip with the aid of a tuning fork is a good point to consider; mine that I have used in the past is a 512 cycles, note C. **The recording of sound telepathy may be accomplished with a tuning fork with multiple synchronized overlapping recording tracks.**

Advancing with Sound Flip

As a novice a person must be in control of the sound producing device and then in time he or she does not need to regulate the noise-making device and progresses to a distance of 3 meters, which is the first hands free stage. Running water is one of the many ways of progressing with sound Flip.

Running water is easy to sound Flip with and also an easy way to learn some advanced telepathy progression technique. I spent a month in jail living in a six man cellblock section that had private cell units; each unit containing one man, a bed, and one sink that was molded onto the top of the toilet. This was the only time in my life I spent time in jail for being not guilty of anything but that is another story altogether so we will skip the circumstances leading to my incarceration and move on to the Flip part. It worked out for the best because I got to practice shithouse psychology in jail.

The men in jail learned foot talking from me and were excellent at it. Now each cell had a private toilet and just about every one of them was slightly out of repair as happens with a lot of jail toilets. The industrial toilets did not shut off on cue like they were suppose to and the toilets continued to run water for a couple of minutes after they were flushed. This discrepancy in the toilets gave an extended time to **sound Flip words into this swirling water's noise.** You have to remember that jail is real boring and at times full of silliness for entertainment to pass the time and invent laughter.

At first the men talked sound Flip with the swirling water as they had their hand on the toilet's sink washing their hands and this is no big deal as it affords some degree of manipulation with the sound-producing device by touching it. Then the men began to walk away from the swirling water up to about 3 meters away and still talk sound Flip with the water's flush swirling noise. The cell block prisoners' hands were free from touching or manipulation of the sound device at 3 meters away and this was the next level up progressing towards "Pure Flip" with the hands free from touching the sound producing device.

One thing peculiar here was that this swirling water was the only sound the men in jail could Flip with at a distance without touch control. These men could not Flip with the buffer motor noise for waxing the floor, the drill motor noise doing repairs, the fan motor sound, or any other sound at a distance without touching it for some reason. The men could also sound Flip words well when taking a shower but they manipulated this sound by the splashing of the water on their bodies and rotating a little.

So we now see that as a person gets proficient at manipulating a sound device with telepathy, they may begin to give up the touching control and begin to increase the distance from the noise-making device up to about 3 meters for most people in the beginning of the "hands free" stage.

Truckers are also very adept at talking Flip with their diesel engines and may also walk away from their truck's motor for a distance of up to ten feet still using the diesel motor's noise to Flip words with. The diesel motor of a semi truck gives off a distinct rhythm that makes it very easy to use for sound Flip. In time a person may sound Flip with the noise on and around the highway, even across the width of the median using the sound of the vehicles moving in the opposite direction of your travel, approximately 100 meters. Cars and trucks on the same side traffic as your direction of travel emit sounds as they pass close by your vehicle while passing you and also offer an opportunity to sound Flip with hands free.

If the push out of the word syllable from your conscious mind is not synchronized properly with the sound rhythm, the telepathic word communication will not sound clear when perceived. With just a little more concentration focused on the synchronization of the sound with your conscious thought these discrepancies or fuzziness of the sound telepathy communication will clear up.

So now we have the truckers with diesel motors at ten feet away without any control of the sound making device only using their minds to control the sound; likewise the people in jail talking with the water in the industrial toilets at the same distance of approximately 3 meters. Both have advanced up the ladder of Flip telepathy towards the "Pure" stage by being in the hands free telepathy stage.

It may be noted here that if a person was to tie a long string or wire to a motor and then back up 50 meters pulling the string tight as they backed away they would be able to feel the vibrations of the motor through the wire and this auxiliary helper of the wire would give confidence to the mind for future hands free sound telepathy.

Foot Talking

Talking telepathy with one's feet is accomplished by stepping out syllables of word as one walks. **First you form a word in your conscious mind. Then concentrating on this word you break the word into syllables. Next you imagine pushing a syllable of word out of your conscious mind into the precise beat of a footstep as it contacts the ground.**

In time a person might step out and communicate more than one syllable per step but in the beginning let us just use one syllable of word per footstep. Noise does not have to be produced while walking to communicate your thoughts with telepathy. Extra noise such as hard soled shoes walking on hard floors, gravel, or crunchy snow, does however make it a lot easier to relate ones thoughts with footsteps. The louder the noise emitted from under your footstep, the easier the Flip is to synchronize but noise is not a requirement for foot talking synchronization.

Foot talking can be interpreted as far as the eye can differentiate the time the foot comes into contact with the earth. Usually this foot talking is perceivable out to the range of about 400 meters. With the aid of a telescope I was able to read foot talking at a distance of 2 miles; it remains to be seen what the limits of a telescope are for interpreting foot talking.

Foot talking can only be interpreted live and in person. Attempts to read foot talking from television, or the movies, will only result in mental confusion. Leave these mediums alone for any kind of mental telepathy as there is a time delay and this prevents exact synchronization.

I am pretty sure I am the creator of foot talking, yet in the beginning I even had trouble believing that people 100 meters away were interpreting my "feet talking". I had never read or ever heard of people talking with their feet before. As I practiced my first steps of telepathy I found it hard to believe and I myself required a lot of verification from other people vocally that I was actually communicating with my feet.

People in my neighborhood would give me vocal repetition of what my footsteps were communicating with telepathy by talking to me from their front porches as I went by walking on the sidewalk. I then began experimenting more with foot talking, walking around the downtown area and also in the local neighborhood where I was living.

Soon all the neighborhood people began to take interest in my foot talking. It was such a fascinating thing that everybody took an interest in the telepathy with my footsteps that observed it. In fact, it was unbelievable to perform foot talking and witness it in the very beginning. Foot talking seemed to be such a miracle; yet also a natural thing for people to do. Everyone expressed a little astonishment at first and then in a few minutes after witnessing it they would begin to totally accept the new practice of foot talking and start performing it themselves.

After I had a firm grip on foot talking I started to consider its future ramifications and what affect it would have on childrens' psyche. **I was going to consider foot talking effects on the human mind for a few months before unleashing it on the world.** It seemed to be the most intelligent thing to do as well as the correct philosophical choice for the time being. I was concerned in the very beginning that foot talking might undermine a child's sense of reality. I did not want to be responsible for hurting childrens' minds with this new invention of mine, foot talking. As days wore on I the inventor proved to be the only one afraid of foot talking affecting childrens' minds.

Once I showed some of the local neighborhood parents foot talking they all decided to go forward with foot talking mental telepathy regardless of my warnings. I tried to get them to refrain from teaching children foot talking for about 6 months but the parents were not concerned about the possibility of any harmful consequences to their children's mind. Some of the parents began to spread the news of foot talking by telephone to other people in cities far from me. It caught on like wildfire to whoever became acquainted with the new thing called foot talking. Parents all decided to ignore my advice of studying the idea of foot talking for a few months, taking no time to observe this new telepathy for any harmful effects on a child's mind. Therefore against my advice the parents all decided to go forward with foot talking regardless of my opinions.

I now joined the public in foot talking as it always seemed that they all preferred talking to me initiating the mental telepathy foot talking and I responded back with more foot talking. They seemed to think I was the key in synchronizing a novice person's mind in foot talking although we all were novices at this time. So after a month I just gave in as everyone around me was talking with his or her feet to me. At this point the cat was out of the bag; the thing that I had created was out of my control now. Although disregarding a test period for foot talking, parents did however always pass on my warning about validating the children with vocal repetition of what the child was trying to convey with their feet especially the younger children.

Note: it is now over 10 years later, and thousands of children have been taught foot talking and I have heard of no ill effects at all to date.

There came a huge breakthrough occurring about a month into this foot talking for justification of the risks involved in parents teaching their children this foot talking. I noticed that children were not ashamed to talk about the various forms of child abuse or anything else for that matter with their feet. **I was truly amazed that children loved to talk with their feet and they were not ashamed to talk nasty or shameful things. Who would have guessed this great surprise?** This was one of the reasons parents decided to teach their children foot talking regardless of my warnings or what the risks might be.

Children were walking and talking with their footsteps in the mall, downtown, school, and every other place on the planet earth and saying terrible immoral things without a hint of guilt or embarrassment. A great tool for exposing child abuse was born. Any small risk associated with foot talking was of no importance to these parents when they became aware of this potential to help children. The dam had now broke for releasing foot talking mental telepathy to the world. There was absolutely no way to stop parents from teaching children mental telepathy with their footsteps at this point. I went right along with the public now practicing foot talking always issuing warnings about validating people especially their small children.

Walking and thinking are two normal basic functions of the human being and I think the natural combination of the two with telepathy will work to be a great tool for mankind into the future.

Children will include mental telepathy in their world from the beginning of their lives. To all of us adults this mental telepathy is an impossible mental task that has been somewhat added to our normal reality. I had worked a little with mental telepathy with sound before this foot talking. Foot talking however helped to give us a solid hold onto the reality of mental telepathy by being a more natural daily occurrence without the aid of artificial auxiliary devices. **Foot talking along with sound Flip gave mankind the tangible validation needed for a strong foundation that forms a reference point to move ever forward in the field of mental telepathy.**

At first I was using a small amount of sound with the medium of loose gravel under my footsteps while foot talking. Over time I learned to communicate word syllables with my footsteps without the aid of sound. In a short time the noise began to separate itself into a separate entity that could stand alone or be combined with other forms of mental telepathy communication.

I started using mental telepathy with sound around July of 1996 while driving semi-truck using the sound of the diesel motor as it was engine braking through its dual exhaust pipes. Although I practiced mental telepathy with the noise of the diesel motor on and off over a period of 6 months I did not realize what I was doing at that time. It never dawned on me that I was injecting silent conscious thoughts into the engine brake sound by telepathy synchronization. All the people on the highway perceived this sound telepathy totally correct laughing and giving verbal repetition of what was being Flipped with the motor braking noise of my semi-truck but none of us realized that this was sound telepathy in its beginning stage back in 1996.

When I started talking with my feet in March of 98, I then realized we were practicing mental telepathy with sound back in 96. The foot talking solidified my earlier experiences with sound telepathy and enlightened me as to what I had done before with sound Flip. As we see in this former example I was practicing telepathy yet I was not aware of it. This book makes all the people who read it aware of mental telepathy's existence and the possible gifts that they also may possess themselves.

Some people with mental thinking problems and some normal people just have a very hard time with vocal expression. These same handicapped people enjoy communicating with foot talking and a lot of these people who are taciturn vocally will talk with their feet all day long. **Some mentally impaired people will not admit to, or talk about their mental problems with vocal explanations.** Yet same these people are more than happy to explain their mental problems by walking by a person and talking with their feet no matter how shameful or embarrassing their problems may be. I have observed this habit of mentally impaired people explaining themselves to me with foot talking many times. For some of these mentally handicapped people this foot talking is a great tool to finally be able to communicate with people around them; especially talking about their problems. I would like to add that sound Flip is another technique also beneficial for communicating problems or simply communicating thoughts.

Some homeless people do not communicate to the people around them. With the advent of foot talking these same taciturn homeless people do have the means to communicate with the neighborhood. It makes the people of the neighborhood more comfortable and secure when the homeless people of their community or a stranger communicates their thoughts and intentions as they pass through the neighborhood talking with their feet. The homeless people seem to feel good about talking to other people with this foot talking telepathy, or perhaps sound Flip.

One day I was privileged to witness a poignant experience on a city bus involving foot talking and motion talking. I observed a person on the bus who had some handicap that made the man's body twitch terrible bad. Every 10 or 20 seconds the man would twitch. He knew who I was and knew I was responsible for foot talking going on around town. He seemed to be talking to me with his twitches, which really is not that amazing to me but he conveyed to me with these twitches that he could not speak except to manage hello. As the man got off the bus he crossed in the pedestrian crosswalk in front of the bus and started to talk with his feet. Tears were in my eyes realizing that I had cured a small part of the world. It gave me a great feeling that I had made a great contribution to the world. I knew the telepathy would go a lot further but this incident gave me some satisfaction for my labors early in the development of Flip. This is just one experience that points to man's intense desire to communicate with others. **Although everybody has an intrinsic urge to communicate some people do not have the ability to be vocal for whatever the reason.**

Now there came a wonderful break through about a year and half after the start of foot talking for the severely mentally handicapped people. Just when I was done writing this Foot Talking section I observed a minor miracle. For two weeks I worked helping people that were declared mentally insane. These people cannot keep a constant train of thought no matter how hard they tried. These insane people could not express one sentence of related thought in the course of a day. These insane people talked complete nonsense and this nonsense was usually not related to any reasonable expression of thought. In essence a complete scattering of silly thoughts, of which none were pertinent to the environment or the people around them.

Although these insane people were incapable of any expression of vocal clear thought, I was able to teach them foot talking and they were all able to keep a clear train of thought as long as they were walking. I could not believe it but all the insane people were talking clear thought and these same insane people knew that they were making sense now. I observed these same people about ten of them for about two weeks. It never changed; these people talking complete unrelated nonsense constantly with their vocals to me. Then they would get up foot talking and they would keep a clear train of thought every time they practiced foot talking. Once I taught these insane people foot talking they never stopped practicing it. These insane people loved this foot talking. They all realized that they were back in reality when they practiced Foot Talking. The Foot Talking was of course slow (one syllable of word per step) but it was totally coherent. I do hope it holds true for all mentally handicapped people as it gives them a ray of hope.

I would like to share another interesting experience with foot talking. It was a rainy night in Portland, Oregon somewhere between 7 and 9 p.m. during the winter months making it dark at this time of night. I had just finished a late night supper of spaghetti and was headed back to my motel for the night. I could see a man foot talking up the block about 50 meters away. The man impressed me on how well he was expressing himself with foot talking from this distance. We both had hooded raincoats on and when the man approached me he asked me directions about a certain street address. Much to my surprise the man was very difficult to understand. The man was Oriental with very little English capabilities. Yet this same man had from over 50 meters away in the dark rainy night conveyed to me that he was talking perfectly clear English with no indication of any foreign accent.

Here is another small curious story about Buddhist Monks in Bangkok, Thailand. I taught about 10 Buddhist Monks foot talking over a period of about five days in downtown Bangkok. These 10 Monks in turn taught all the other Monks in Bangkok foot talking and soon every Monk in Bangkok was talking with their feet as they walked through Bangkok, Thailand. Not a bad form of communication considering these Buddhist never usually talked while walking in public.

The beginning of foot talking is as follows: I was walking down the sidewalk early one morning around 7 am sipping on hot vending machine coffee in a paper cup in my hand and 3 or 4 people were conversing on the corner ahead of me blocking the sidewalk. I cut the corner to avoid the people obstructing my path thereby walking through some gravel and the noise under my step from the crunching gravel made me think of talking with my feet. So I just spontaneously tried to convey "Buenos Dias" with my feet noise to a Mexican man perched on an ornamental boulder on the corner only a few feet from where I was walking on the gravel. This person perceived "Buenos Dias" from the crunching gravel noise under my feet and returned "Buenos Dias" vocally. Foot talking was now born much to my amazement, April 1998 in Phoenix, Arizona.

Although foot talking is new everybody is able to pick up on it before they know anything about it. My friends and I were foot talking on a construction job site for about 20 minutes before a new man completely unaware of the existence of foot talking caught on and recognized we were talking with our feet. The man exclaimed: "Oh I get it! You're talking with your feet". It was extremely funny but it also proved that the man was able to read our feet performing telepathy without any prior knowledge of foot talking.

The other day I was discouraged with this nonsense called foot talking. The following day I was in the downtown shopping district of Fresno, California among the many shops along the promenade of the city. Some children greeted me with their feet and I greeted them back with foot talking. Some of the children got excited and started running around helping me recite ABC's and spelling three letter words all over the immediate downtown area in the promenade. I went from the state of mind of a doubting Thomas to having a minor mania attack about foot talking curing the world.

As a person goes out around people say downtown, the mall, etc., their mind begins to crave communication with other people around them. Usually all the people that surround us in these crowds in the downtown area are not spoken to. This is where foot talking comes in handy for the human mind as a communication release. You are usually walking through the crowd anyway so why not use your walking as a way to converse now and then informally to others? Normally you would not greet these people but with the invention of foot talking, greeting these people becomes a perfectly natural thing occurring at the mall or pedestrian crosswalk. I think in time that greeting people like this will become a totally socially acceptable thing as it is a form of casual communication and if need be easily ignored.

Motion Talking

When I began to teach people the art of foot talking, motion talking also began to take shape at the same time. Although foot talking is a form of motion talking it has a different synchronization point, which are the feet striking the earth. In motion talking the synchronization point is done with change of direction, abrupt stoppages, or touching. People use hand motions and arm movements along with using their legs to motion Flip.

Riding a bicycle synchronizing the full down stroke extension of the leg with word syllables pushed out of your conscious mind is an easy technique. Pantomime may also be used in conjunction with motion telepathy. Even mouth gestures and blinking of the eyes can be used to transmit telepathy with motion. Like I mentioned before; foot talking is accomplished perfectly the first time attempted by all people. In addition motion talking can be accomplished with just a little more effort, the synchronization part being slightly more difficult.

Pantomime motions will take on new meaning when accompanied with Flip communicating precise syllables of word along with acting motions. I am hoping that motion Flip will help deaf people in communicating with ***sign language*** that is perfect for their hand movements and also helps accentuate Lip Sync.

Note: Lip Sync is nothing more than moving your mouth and lips with a bit of exaggeration trying to form words but without speaking any sound. This helps the internal conscious mind to think and hear the telepathy word projection a little clearer before pushing it out to others, and the Lip Sync is also normally used for the deaf.

Public Speakers will benefit by adding motion Flip to stress important points in their speeches. Many public speakers use their hands to hold attention and emphasize a point. These speakers could synchronize important words from their speeches in their conscious mind with hand motions. Not only will motion Flip help speakers get their point across but also put up somewhat of a defense against people who will be masters of Flip that are attacking them. These masters of Flip will be appearing on the public scene shortly. It is human nature to have a bad day and try to take your stress out on someone else through telepathy. Although it goes against ethics these master telepathists will on occasion mess with other people's minds, to a small degree for the most part but you can expect to be messed with sometime in the future with Flip if you are a frequent public speaker. Practicing Motion Flip in Speeches or the Defense against outside intrusion requires increased concentration and practice. A person will continue to get more proficient at Motion Flip and the defense against telepathy over a period of 6 months.

Even the audience clapping may be a sound Flip from the entire opinion of your audience or the clapping Flip may have the conscious words of a single person controlling and overriding the opinion of the audience's mental telepathy by interjecting his or her own thoughts into the clapping sound. A master telepathist will control all the clapping sound no matter what the entire audience wants to say with sound Flip. So the Flip must be differentiated and sometimes ignored. I will begin to discuss advanced Flip later in this book, as for now just be aware that these highly skilled telepathists with utmost control of thoughts exist and will appear in the near future in increasing numbers. These masters of Flip can use a speaker's hand motion and voice to interject their own thoughts with motion telepathy or sound Flip. This can be distracting but as I said before once familiar with what goes on with mental telepathy the shock value is lost confusing you less and thereby easier to overlook and defense.

A master telepathist could interject his nasty thoughts into a large audience clapping such as a Congressional Meeting. After a few times of doing "nasty things" a master will feel silly doing this and eventually this will lead the ending of this unethical behavior. In addition the world conscience should begin to give him nightmares in their mind if the master exhibits any inappropriate behavior for a great length of time. Also close friends and people in close proximity with the master telepathist will eventually figure out who the culprit of this nasty telepathy is. Nasty telepathy should just be ignored if possible preventing validation that would enable the perpetrator to become more proficient.

Validation Responses

A person that practices mental telepathy in any form should have his or herself validated by a friend. The best way to validate telepathy is by other people verifying by vocalization what an originator (the transmitter) of telepathy is trying to communicate. Validating should be of major concern here when teaching any technique of Flip.

It would be next to impossible to keep your children from talking with their feet or using sound Flip if they so wished. Some parents consider foot talking a gift from God being that it combines two naturally occurring things i.e. thinking and walking. Still other parents think foot talking is a way to prevent child abuse and are adamant about its instruction to their children. Children playing with your own children will also be instructing your child in play and at school in sound Flip, motion Flip, and foot talking.

This is why my opinion of teaching children simple forms of telepathy or yours for that matter are of no consequence here. A lot of children are going to be practicing telepathy at school so let's all be on the safe side by validating them when we can thereby keeping their young minds healthy. I think preschoolers should be validated every word at this very young age.

Some parents might consider some children too young to teach foot talking, motion Flip, or sound Flip. Needless to say when the young children enter the school system they will encounter these basic forms of telepathy through socializing with the other children. At this elementary age a lot of mothers are going to teach their children foot talking to help prevent child abuse. Children are not embarrassed to admit the various forms of child abuse with foot talking. In fact a lot of mothers are going to teach their children to speak embarrassing things concerning child abuse with telepathy. **Parents will be instructing their children to practice saying terrible scenarios whether it occurs or not with telepathy as a sort of de-**

sensitivity training for a time in the future when it may be actually needed when and if child abuse really occurs.

How much a first grader needs to be validated I the author does not really know. The parent cannot be around their child at school and the teacher cannot watch all the children on the playground resulting in a lot less verification of what is being said with children's foot talking, motion Flip, or sound Flip. It would be best if the parent instructed their child to validate other children on occasion. The children will most likely acknowledge another child's foot talking with more foot talking. The other forms of telepathy may also be used to validate a different type of Flip. **One example would be foot talking validated by another child on the playground with the sound Flip of a bouncing rubber ball.** Another child would simply validate this foot talking by returning the word or words Flipped with the sound Flip of a bouncing ball. The playground in the near future with all these children bouncing balls, motion Flipping and foot talking will be full of telepathy communication of all sorts.

Now adults in my opinion need validation about once a month. Again, to tell the absolute truth I really do not know the amount of validation needed to keep a person's mind healthy by trying to prevent the undermining of their reality by the practicing of this Flip. I am just making suggestions here on what I think is best for everyone.

To reiterate, all a person has to do to validate another person's mental telepathy is to tell them what they are saying by repeating the sender's telepathy; this done best with vocal repetition but other forms of telepathy may also be used for a return validation response. Vocal repetition may not always be available as people are embarrassed to repeat telepathy with vocals at times. The non-vocal example here was validating foot talking with sound Flip. The more frequently you validate telepathy the better it will make the sender's proficiency. This gives return confirmation of telepathy to the sender and the sender's mind really knows that he or she is actually capable of communicating this way.

A parent might endorse foot talking and say no to the rest of mental telepathy like sound talking telepathy. I do not see any problem with picking and choosing or totally ignoring this new stuff altogether if you deem it detrimental to you or your child. You just need to keep in mind the majority of children will be practicing Flip at school and your child will learn mental telepathy through these other children regardless of what parents' or teachers' opinions are.

With the writing of this book people will have the validation needed to solidify their confidence and move forward expanding thought transference. **The book "FLIP" itself is a strong validation for the human mind and you did well reading it and one better if in your possession for a tangible validation by knowing the book exists in your home.**

Suicide Prevention

Mental problems affecting a person's mind have to be talked about to relieve stress and guilt. A person may not be able to relate mental problems to a significant other with a normal conversation of eye-to-eye confrontation as this is too scary a scenario for some individuals. A child may be afraid to admit shameful or intimate incidents to their parents. An individual wishes to discuss his or her problems with their family but sometimes this is way too threatening for a lot of people with a normal conversation, especially children.

A person may use foot talking around family or friends to discuss their problems or may take a ride in a car discussing his or her problems with the sound Flip of the car. Taking a ride in a car sounds a little unusual but this sound Flip with a car is a very natural thing that occurs on a daily basis. If the person with the mental problem is driving a car the sound Flip is easy and really a pleasure to do. **So if a person has a problem that is too threatening to discuss face to face, simply take a nice ride in your car with your friend communicating with the sound telepathy of the vehicle.**

Other types of sound telepathy may used for relating mental problems. Some of the types are playing a musical instrument such as a guitar and sound Flipping your personal grief or perhaps playing sports such as bouncing a basketball describing your problems to a friend. This all sounds a little ridiculous but this stuff is simple and all works to relieve stress and guilt, which will help prevent suicide attempts. If your friend has another guitar or is playing a game of basketball with you they may respond back with sound Flip thoughts carrying on a therapeutic conversation that is non-threatening.

It is also possible to go for a walk in the park and discuss your personal problems foot talking or maybe wading through the water of the surf on the beach with sound Flip added.

Again we need to mention that if you are a close friend or family member you should be able to pick up some ***mental drift*** or ***transparency*** of your friends sick mind through this simple form of telepathy. Do not deny these ESP possibilities exist; they are for real in the present world and may assist you in helping your friend or children prevent suicide.

These simple telepathy techniques will help to prevent suicide by releasing stress and guilt from mental problems through communication and help keep this communication path flowing between people. The difference between serious mental problems, serious sickness, and simple irritating problems, all are divided by a very fine line. Telepathy stress relief will help keep a person on the safe side of this fine line and stop this serious problem of suicide from occurring.

The telepathy techniques described in this book do provide a catharsis or drawing out of stress or guilt, or grief from the memories thereby reducing or eliminating irrational cognitive thinking and depression that leads to thoughts of suicide.

I would also like to point out that if a person practices basic telepathy skills they will communicate with many others and telepathy will increase their self-esteem helping to stop death thoughts.

Ignoring Flip

I do not think that any of the forms of mental telepathy mentioned in this book will ever go away in our society. On the contrary I think that mental telepathy is going to grow in usage over time. A person has to accept the fact that they are going to encounter telepathy techniques in a public environment sooner or later. You have to also be aware of the fact that Flip is going to be the only convenient and spontaneous way for some handicapped people to communicate with and they will always be practicing this telepathy over the course of their lifetime in the public realm for communication.

Once you have learned Flip or become familiar with it you may choose to ignore it completely. The Flip is not going to be for everyone in the 21st century. Comprehending what Flip is will enable you as an individual to defense it and if you choose, totally ignore it. Even if you love this mental telepathy you will not want to pay attention to all of it especially all the communication going on in large crowds.

So by not concentrating on other peoples Flip and by forcing your mind into a different rhythm or image scenario, you will help to overlook somebody else's attempt at unwanted Flip communication with you. If your mind gets too overloaded with stimulus it will normally simply begin to ignore Flip on its own. If a person really gets overloaded with stress thoughts from other people's mind transference then I think a short nap will alleviate this stress maybe 20 minutes or they may try void meditation as described in this book.

You all need to be advised that a lot of people will be trying very hard to master this mental telepathy. **The Flip is a source of fun, a way for power, domination, and a natural way for the human mind to want to communicate with others. We all know people that love to talk and never seem to shut up, the same holds true for the Flip.**

In general I think mankind is a naturally mean animal said to be approximately 3.5

million years old by fossil dating. And of these 3.5 million years of killing things for survival I would guess that mankind has been somewhat civilized for 5,000 years. This few thousand years of civilization is a mere drop in the bucket for mankind when compared to the total time of man's existence on this planet earth. Mankind is inherently mean and aggressive by nature. If mankind were not inherently mean there would be no need for any law enforcement, prison or war. Of course in most human situations intelligence wins out against primitive human violence. This violent behavior does however exist on this planet in large amounts as exhibited by numerous wars occurring at this very moment of your reading this book.

It is human nature for man to be aggressive in some form. When humans cannot express their aggressive behaviors then this thwarted desire will often turn to silliness. Most often if silliness is continued it will escalate into hurtful humor sometimes escalating further into aggressive behavior. We all extract goodness from people at times so I don't want to be a total Cynic on the capabilities of human social behavior. I am trying to point out here that telepathy is a perfect tool for mean people to practice their art of bullying and we all know people who live to irritate people. **If you perceive a mean Flip you should try to ignore it. If you acknowledge a mean Flip it will make the executor a little better at it and also encourage this type of behavior from them in the future.**

Occasionally a mean person will get a lucky shot in; in fact everybody will at different times pull off great works of Flip communication at random. People will unlikely hit home runs of great quality telepathy on a regular basis, when they do just be prepared to ignore these attacks even though they may startle you. All people have pent up frustrations that build to the boiling point and they will be looking for ways to vent this stress. Flip is a path for the human mind to take when overloaded with stress and vocals are blocked; communication being a way to relieve stress and naturally flip is a way to be normal again by venting this overload of stress.

We just want to be aware of people with *__evil intentions__* practicing mental telepathy for whatever the reason and not respond to these with return validation that will increase their unethical behavior even more. I, the author do not want to scare people away from mental telepathy. The Flip will probably be one of the best things that ever happened to mankind but maybe not totally acceptable in our lifetime for everyone.

Precautions also must be taken not to be obsessed with telepathy to the point where you have no control of the input of other people's thoughts constantly bombarding your brain when you are busy with your own train of thought. I think that children growing up with mental telepathy will be able to filter out Flip just like any multiple conversations happening in a crowd of people and do just fine.

Dream Suggestion

When a person is sleeping they may have images or other concepts suggested to them with live vocals by a person who is awake and in close proximity or within hearing range of the sleeping person. Some ordinary people are capable of creating fantastic images and achieve problem solving in their sleep through suggestion by another consciously awake person or possibly by a descriptive voice tape recording. Naturally most of these dream fabrications are not remembered unless the person's conscious is awakened during the dream or shortly after the dream.

This might take a few months of practice or a person that possesses a little telepathic skill might make an easy time of it. Many images suggested during sleep and then formed by the dreaming mind are of a beautiful nature and are full of fantastic detail, more vivid and complex than normal.

The ordinary subliminal dream tapes sold cannot be that good and in fact what is subliminal about most of these tapes? I never could figure out these countless number of subliminal tapes sold in stores. Is there a voice beyond normal hearing only picked up by the pre-conscious? Relaxation tapes I can see the validity of as many of these are very soothing with ocean waves and trickling water, but subliminal I think they are not.

I do think there is good possibility of doing good things with these particular dream suggestion tapes used during sleep if they are carefully constructed. I think the tape has to be more descriptive for one thing, in colors, details of physical construction, and other detailed appearances of the suggested concept. **Normally the brain dreams while in R.E.M. (rapid eye movement) but with a live voice suggesting concepts, dreams begin immediately when a live voice begins to talk to the individual occurring as soon as he or she falls asleep.** Emotions, touch, smells, sounds and many other things may be added to the fabrication of the problem solving dream suggestion, all totally capable from the dreaming brain.

It is possible that a person would better trust their own voice in a tape they have personally constructed themselves then a stranger's voice in a store bought tape. **Even a little better is the live voice of another awake person, which seems to be more powerful and effective in penetrating and manipulating the sleeping brain more so than a recorded tape.**

So-called subliminal recordings that are played during dream sleep, work by suggesting various things during dream sleep and should be handled carefully regardless. I have heard many lectures and debates from Psychology Professors of leading American colleges on the subject of subliminal tapes. Most Psychology Professors are against these recordings because they view them as ineffectual. I was inclined to agree with these men as they were PhD professionals from the most prestigious colleges; until I started developing telepathy skills.

It seems as though dreams are not viewed in the conscious gallery but probably in the pre-conscious zone as the conscious seems to be in a resting state and shut down. Should the dream be too violent or excessively emotionally charged then the conscious will be awakened automatically by this highly emotional or threatening situation in the dream. These threatening situations in dreams necessitate the conscious awareness that helps in remedying the situation to a less threatening or less emotional one thus awakening the person from dream sleep.

Most of a person's normal dreaming is the vacating of trash thoughts from the short term memory into the vast universe, which is the pre-conscious zone.

Although a lot of the dream content may not be remembered by the dreaming person when awakening, fantastic creations may be achieved during dreaming through suggestion from a person that is awake. Most of the dream will be remember if the person is awakened when suggestion is done. It is probably best to suggest to a dreaming person for 2-5 minutes and then awaken the dreaming person so as to view the previous dream suggestion topic. The dream occurs extremely rapidly yet the mind picks up all details and at times the topic or problem is realized or solved in a matter of seconds.

Other people in a ***summation telepathy meditation group*** with their eyes closed may view these individuals dream creations very easily as they are actually occurring inside the dreaming individual's mind that the group is keyed upon. This observation of the dreaming individuals mind by the group is made a little easier if the person that is dreaming is a master at telepathy. The master's telepathic mind facilitates the group members to enter these new internal mind dimensions of telepathy while the master is dreaming. The summation group observes the individuals dream scenario as it occurs and suggest problem solving constructions using the dreaming individuals dreaming mind as a door opener for these infinite new ***internal mind dimensional doors*** that make available infinite resources for dream construction suggested by the awake group members. It is possible that the others in summation telepathy following the dream may add other mind resources to the dream construction.

I have not tried it but it may be possible to have a group of sleeping individuals to work with a dream suggested to them by one awake person (narrator) in order for them to interconnect for fantastic dream constructions and problem solving through summation. A narrator could detail and build these dreams among this room of people with one person in the room being a master of telepathy; the suggestion group all sleeping together except the narrator who is describing the dream scene. All the people in the room dreaming should see the master telepathist's dream fabrication altogether as one and may also add details and parts to the dream sequence. The narrator when finished with the dream scene needs to slowly wake the dreamers up together to a conscious state; the dreamers will all remember the dream now and begin talking about what they have seen or fabricated and record this now in writing.

These dream constructions are fantastic with enriched colors and other sense perceptions that are unattainable in normal awake individuals. One such group of people could be a team of 10 top scientists doing dream suggestion together to cure H.I.V. or cancer. This gathering of scientists doing dream suggestion appears to be a little far-fetched but at present this is easy to do and most likely an innate ability of the human mind. After five minutes of dream suggestion the scientists need to be awakened and the progress recorded. If willing, this group of scientists could continue these dream suggestion sessions indefinitely being woke up once or twice during the night for feedback recording.

During sleep the conscious mind of the dreaming individual is shut down and the only time it will remember a dream is if the conscious wakes up during the dream. The conscious upon awakening views the part of dream that is closest in proximity to the ***conscious threshold viewing window***. Other parts of the dream that have occurred minutes earlier are already almost out of focus of the conscious and are faint to view and hard to recognize as ***the dream moves away very rapidly through the pre-conscious zone***. Dreams are not meant to be remembered; they are meant to be forgotten as vacated trash. This illustration of dreams racing by and away from the ***conscious threshold viewing window*** **is the same as Albert Einstein's Doppler Effect**. Doppler Effect is like a speeding train coming to your location point on the train track from a point in the distance. The train increases in size and clarity along with sound as it approaches your location point on the train track (same as conscious threshold viewing window). The train is largest, clearest, and loudest when directly in front of your observation point. As the train moves away it diminishes in size, detail clarity, sound, and total recognition; same as a person's conscious awaking during a dream.

During a time of various sicknesses a person's ***conscious threshold barrier*** is weak, many times from fever or stress. **When the conscious threshold barrier is**

weak the pre-conscious leaks disorganized junk into the conscious a bit causing semi-awake nightmares during this time of fever or stress. A mother speaking to her child during these types of sick nightmares may help lessen them as the speaking and possibly telepathy summation of the mother helps strengthen the conscious threshold barrier wall of the child and may also orient the dreams of the sick child to a more tranquil topic thereby soothing the child.

A person may be psychologically harmed if a nearby awake person spoke bad things to them during sleep if the person is within audible range. As they sometimes say; you do not want to sleep with the enemy as they could do psychological harm. Consequently people should not be abused in their sleep by others as this is unethical and a very sadistic attack. I suppose an agreement with someone to do this sleep suggestion would be ok if they both understood the content to be suggested during the sleep session. Occasional nice things that are said by another awake person to their sleeping partner probably would be in order with no harm. Saying I love you would tend to create a good feeling when the sleeping person's conscious awakes.

Hypnosis - Under hypnosis it might be an improvement to use telepathy to try to break through into the memories for therapy. The mental telepathy might be less threatening to the defenses of the brain that resist normal communication or it might possible to fool the brain enabling Flip telepathy to penetrate and communicate directly with the memories for healing instructions. And again simple live voice suggestion may be more beneficial here.

False Memories - I have personally had thousands of dream suggestions done by neighborhood watch that have attempted to plant false memories in my mind but not a single suggestion was remembered as a false memory although the dreams were remembered as true implants and not actual occurrences. Elaborate dreams and problem solving may be fabricated by dream suggestion but these dream fabrications are totally differentiated by the mind as present occurrences and not past true events.

If the subject is a child or mentally handicapped person I think it would be possible to implant false memories by dream suggestion and care must be taken here.

Addiction

Mental telepathy seems to be a naturally inherent thing that has laid dormant over time appearing to be already pre-programmed for the human mind. The need to communicate is very strong in the human species practiced in whatever means is available or convenient. **Most of us are truly addicted to talking vocally for information or just for the fun of it. This same addiction for communicating vocally will pull at a person's mind to practice communicating with mental telepathy.**

Flip communication has the advantage of being an informal way to greet people in the world. One example would be foot talking in a large city in the downtown area while walking through the crowds of people. Normally a person would not walk through a crowd of people at the train or bus station conversing as they go but with the knowledge of Flip they will.

The need to communicate begins to build in the brain accumulating energy until it finds a portal through vocalizing and when vocalizing is blocked then mental telepathy will provide a convenient outlet for this communication energy. Foot talking and sound Flip along with the other forms of mental telepathy provide an easy and informal way of releasing this energy pent up inside our brains to communicate with other people.

Many of the components of the human mind have needs and wants that demand to be conveyed to the outside world through communication. There is the **need to be silly,** for no matter how old an individual is they always want to duplicate a ten-year-old's mentality on occasion. The **need to be aggressive** or mean, bipedal Homo Sapiens are said to be about 3.5 million years old and practically all this time was spent killing animals and humans for survival. There is the **need to be domineering** or a leader over other people providing the feeling of power. In addition there is a

strong desire for sex. We should also throw the very important needs of **food and shelter** in here. All these needs and various less important ones are pulling hard at an individual's brain to communicate these wishes with other people and this leads to tremendous pressure on the mind to talk about them to other people. When talking is blocked these human needs will begin to build and put pressure on the mind to communicate these wants. **Once the human mind knows that it has another convenient form of release in the form of mental telepathy it will constantly go for this release when the communication energy builds and normal vocalizing is delayed or blocked.**

Once the Flip sucks you in and most likely it will hook the vast majority of the population in time, it will be hard to drop it cold turkey. I suggest you practice a little self-control right from the start with mental telepathy. With all this Flip beginning to spread around a person has to learn to ignore his or her feelings of obligation to return all communication directed at them with Flip. **Most people do not realize that they are addicted to returning all verbal communication in public.** It seems only right to return the favor of a greeting in public. In the future with the practicing of mental telepathy especially in the big city the large amount of people will just overload your mind at times increasing stress and leaving less time and space for your own thoughts. If you begin listening to the vast amount of Flip in large crowds in the public sphere you will lose continuity of your thoughts.

When a person gets tired of the Flip and seeks total control back to the regular forms of communication it will be then that he or she realizes that they suffer some type of addiction with telepathy. If a person has practiced mental telepathy for a couple of months or more their "conscious will" begins to want its control back and at the same time some kind of energy builds in the back of their mind and keeps trying to push through with Flip communication.

So if a person does not have enough vocal expression the Flip will begin to

win out over the "conscious will" and start communicating with telepathy again automatically releasing pent up communication energy.

Sending and receiving mental telepathy must be stimulating to some pleasure center in the brain as it seems that everyone derives pleasure from participating in this new mind transference stuff. **Telepathy seems to be a pre-programmed doggie bone treat stimulating nerves in the brain; Flipping really is an enjoyable experience for all people and at times comparable to a strong drug addiction.**

Everybody will wake up one morning and say I am free from all this mental telepathy junk and I am going back to normal everyday vocal communication that is a more solid and secure. Then sooner or later you encounter another human being and the need to communicate is too great to repress. The mind begins to put pressure on one's "conscious will". Your "will" might want to resume absolute normal talking leaving this silly Flip alone. However, if the individual does not respond verbally in public with others then pressure to communicate will begin to build in the mind and it will then look to Flip telepathy automatically as a release for this stored communication energy.

The human mind knows that even if it is too shy or proud to speak verbally it has an option to use telepathy for a communication outlet. The human mind wants to be social and communicate always and unfortunately you have taught it another automatic way. Flip in any form gives the brain an opportunity to be social and this is the norm for the human being and there is a good chance the Flip will surface again down the line again and again. Telepathy interconnects minds for communication and the human being loves to be social and communicate. The human mind learns to love telepathy and this telepathy glues minds together for communication.

If any of these forms of mental telepathy described in this book bother your

mind then by all means abandon this stuff. The Flip is a useful tool but it certainly isn't going to be for everybody in our lifetime. I am the inventor of all this jazz but I would certainly not endorse Flip if it seems to bother your mind. Life goes on and some people should take this mental telepathy slow or not at all. I the author and inventor could live without Flip very easily and so could you my friend if telepathy bothers your mind. If you decide to practice Flip I suggest you make one or more days a week free from mental telepathy. This will give one's mind a little self-control over the urge to use telepathy constantly and keep the conscious will in control.

The reading of this book will teach you the techniques of telepathy enabling a person to recognize Flip thereby allowing for the defense or to totally ignore it if so desired.

Note: I have been practicing mental telepathy for 10 years at the writing of this particular edition. This 10 year period has pointed out to me that it is extremely important to learn to ignore telepathy at will. Be careful and practice the ***void technique*** described in the Meditation chapter or other forms of conscious mind control.

Sense of Touch and Vibration

I think one of the nicest thoughts in my book is brushing or combing your child's hair and synchronizing the words I love you with the hair grooming strokes.

Massage, even love bonding may be practiced with mental telepathy through touching the human body and synchronizing syllables of word with each touching motion of the human body. The vibrations of a beating heart can be used likewise to communicate by telepathy touching. A massage vibrating machine may be used to Flip words by regulating the vibrations, this done by touching the vibrating machine and interjecting syllables of soothing words into the rhythmic vibrations of the machine.

Although touching is a sense by itself, it is also done with image projection. Just about everyone can feel my touch image projections. They are faint of course, I imagine pinching somebody's bottom, kissing their cheek or possible tapping their shoulder and somehow they "feel" this telepathy touch projection. To me it seems that they feel this touching Flip a little more than me the sender. I do insects crawling on people sometimes for a joke.

I try not to be too mean when Flipping telepathy concepts at other people's conscious trying to avoid scaring people but the only real fun about this telepathy stuff is the harmless jokes that are almost impossible to refrain from. So have fun and try to remember ethics and do not scare people too much. Touch projection may be used in sports such as mountain climbing using telepathic projection for future hand and foot holds and is explained more in the Sports chapter and also in the Image Projection chapter.

Taste and Smell

The senses of taste and smell are amplified and enriched by using telepathy summation. In a large group setting smell and taste are enriched even more by simple casual group telepathy. One example would be a dinner party with many people pushing forth a group summation amplification of the food's taste and smell that would enhance the foods flavor circulating through all their minds' consciouses simultaneously. While the group is having dinner thinking about aromas and tastes about the food they are eating they also think about pushing the sensations out of their minds with summation Flip. This summation Flip at a dinner party may be aided with soft music playing in the background to synchronize their summation thoughts throughout the dinner party.

Just as smells and tastes can be improved for more enjoyment, they also can be strengthened to increase the offensiveness or bad taste of a substance such as pollution in a city. If a single person smells something bad in a group setting, the whole group will then smell this particular odor and amplify it with Flip for the entire group to smell now with even more strength added to it than would be with a single person.

Primitive Mind

The human primitive mind and likewise the animal mind begin to function right at birth for survival without any higher intelligent thought processes taking place. Another automatic system (the Autonomous) runs the necessary organs such as the lungs and heart to keep us alive without any conscious awareness. The autonomous system and primitive mind are types of mind that perform functions according to physical world stimulus input that is independent of any prior life experiences or learning; which we would consider as pre-programming in the DNA.

The primitive mind of humans that is present at birth in the newborn and also the mature animal mind are both not capable of higher intelligence functions. I have to go along with John Locke's Theory that all humans are born "Tabla Rasa" or just a blank slate that awaits higher learning.

Conscious sensory equipment for input of physical environmental stimulus is present and working at birth in both these types of primitive minds creating attractions and repulsions to various tangible objects for humans and animals. Sensory physical input stimulus such as a moving animal or object, the taste, feel, and smell of a human breast, the texture and darkness of a seashell as sensed by the baby hermit crab are just a few examples of primitive physical sense stimuli available to the newborn child and also the primitive animal mind.

A newborn hermit crab has an immediate attraction for a seashell for protection without using any form of higher intelligence for thinking. The attraction here I think is a sensory-chemical one that matches to the primitive mind of the hermit crab; which seeks out the darkness, texture, and smell of the sea shell. I do not see how it could be anything but a sensory-chemical attraction with a creature that possesses such a small brain. A child psychologist and scientist by the name of Mr. Piaget noticed that newly hatched ducklings' imprint to anything that moves following the first observed moving thing or person thinking this is their mother.

A newborn human baby seeks to suck their mother's breast for nourishment by performing the pre-programmed sucking motions with its mouth initiated solely by its hunger. This sucking motion is present at birth without any learning required by the human baby (a priori). Along with the pre-programmed mouth sucking motion there is physical sense stimuli, being the smell, taste, and feel of their mother's breast for orientation.

These are all examples of attractions and repulsions through sensory and chemical stimulus as provided by the immediate workings of the brains of animals and newborn humans relating to the conscious physical world sensory input and matching them to chemical templates stored in our primitive mind that are pre-programmed by nature a priori.

I would compare these templates to an antibody that can recognize anything foreign in the body and attack. The antibody has an affinity for foreign material identified through a DNA chemical template stored within the simple antibody.

I also think that these simple sensory chemical templates were the key to rapid evolution. The same process that present day antibodies use to rapidly identify and attack a new foreign disease is probably the same basic primitive adaptation process that was also used for rapid evolution in primitive man. This done through stored DNA templates being able to rapidly evolve according to simple pleasant attractions and unpleasant repulsions for the comfort of the primitive human animal.

Mankind did evolve slower in the higher learning processes but once we had an intelligent memory for learning and retaining information we could pass it down to our children through the teachings of the adults. Primitive Man possibly may have had weak mental telepathy summation occurring but I do not really think that there was much of a chance of this occurring in ancient times. Telepathy is a higher form of intelligence thinking that seems to require language skills to function well. Primitive man had no language skills and therefore possessed no telepathy foundation blocks to construct mental telepathy concepts.

<u>Back in ancient times, (in my opinion) there was no collective conscious (connected conscious minds) or in other words telepathy summation occurring</u>. Please remember that conscious is your current thoughts and conscience is morals matched from long term memory.

We have only recently built a working telepathy foundation system with a few proven logic blocks. The living memories of past living humans (dead) might have been picked up on with a little mental drift but I do not think there was any real telepathy in past history as all this mind transference stuff appears to recently have come on the scene and no automatic all knowing living memory was available in the past before this book.

I would like to point out that millions of people have responded to my telepathy as I was working driving semi-truck cross-country through the 48 continental states including many of the large cities of the United States over a period of 4 years. However not a single animal has ever responded to my telepathy after countless tries with various animals. I have only tried once or twice with each animal that I have encountered and I still try once in a while to get animals to respond but so far no response. **It might be possible to work with a monkey or dog from birth for months or years but this remains to be seen as <u>telepathy reception is not pre-programmed in mature animals for instant automatic perception of Flip thoughts as it is in language capable humans</u>.**

Through logical deduction we are able to figure out what part of the human mind is capable of relating to telepathy. Mature Animal minds cannot receive or transmit mental telepathy. Human babies may begin to receive and facilitate neural pathways in the brain for mental telepathy but must learn and memorize over time the practice of mind transference beginning to totally function when speaking language skills appear in the small child.

Telepathy may pass on concept information from the living memories of adults to children but not until higher language functioning is present in the child. Our primitive mind or immature mind does not possess the capability to receive or transmit telepathy because it is a small finite memory incapable of complex thought fabrication only performing sensory-chemical functions of attraction and repulsion.

The fetus or baby may begin to facilitate telepathy neural pathways through sound telepathy or vibrations that may begin totally functioning when communication skills appear in the child. This is to say when language occurs telepathy is definitely present and functioning in the human mind and therefore automatically 100% receptive.

Again my child was never exposed to mental telepathy as a child but if she was she would have had the mental telepathy facilitated in the womb with music and continued with telepathy introduction until talking began. From conception to talking while at the same time being exposed to telepathy will make the telepathy easy to perform for the child when talking appears.

Cognitive Symbols Theory - I always was inclined to agree with the theory that you need words or symbols to create a complete descriptive concept or thought as well as store it in the memories correctly. Mental telepathy sometimes goes a little against this cognitive theory with fuzzy, weak, or incomplete thoughts. It seems that letters or words are not needed for all concepts to originate, the concept being a cognitive event by itself at times intertwined with words and symbols. Sometimes the concept begins to form as an image or feeling without words especially with the addition of telepathy. Cognitive functions are not all preprogrammed and encoded formally with symbols.

Some of these cognitive functions seem to form up with hazy bits and pieces of free-floating debris forming concepts sometimes not needing a word or symbol.

Although not all concepts need words for their formation I think the vast majority of conscious concepts do need words or symbols to increase the volume and clarity of the thought in the conscious gallery. Adding or **assigning words to a particular concept also allows for the conscious to hold the thought in place** for a longer period of time to study and construct the particular thought by the piecing together of numerous simple concepts forming more complex ideas with words. The symbols that you add to a conscious idea also make the concept more efficient by assigning word symbol placeholders for storing in the long term memory.

Helen Keller helps support the theory of cognitive symbols or word assigning for concepts in the following story. The great Helen Keller was struck down with a disease that left her blind and deaf at the age of two before she learned language skills. It wasn't until close to the age of 7 years old that Helen learned words with sign language through her teacher Anne Sullivan. Helen Keller tells the story of how she "thought" before learning words with "wordless sensations" or solely ***stimulus reaction concepts***. The wordless sensations lead to a fuzzy concept as described by Helen. This sounds to me like a subliminal or pre-conscious thought not clearly breaking totally into the conscious focus.

One example Helen Keller described was her mother putting on her hat; Helen then knew she would be feeling the warmth of the sun upon her face soon after the placing of this hat on her head by her mother, which was part of a normal learned stimulus reaction sequence for Helen. Helen did not have words for this sequence of fuzzy concepts only the expectations of upcoming stimulus events after placing the hat on her head.

When Helen's teacher Anne Sullivan taught her the word "water" in her hand with sign language while at the same time touching flowing water, Helen Keller had her first clear thought in her young life at close to 7 years old. Helen said it gave her a kind of "new vision" with the knowledge of cognitive symbols or words that were now attached to the tangible concept by sign language. Without language skills Helen Keller lacked true conscious higher thinking. Thoughts without cognitive symbols do not break the threshold barrier into the conscious with clear focus.

Higher Learning is truly obstructed without words for concepts because without symbols the thought concepts lack enough recognition energy and fail to enter the conscious totally. If these incomplete thoughts do enter the conscious and do not possess enough description they will not be able to be constructed upon to build a larger idea, in addition these thoughts cannot not be held in the conscious for the necessary time to completely construct. These incomplete thoughts will also not be able to be recorded into the memories failing to have the necessary symbols that serve as placeholders in the memory banks.

Meditation by Telepathy

At times my mind becomes cluttered as I pick up on various image telepathy transmissions from others when my eyes are closed. When I am tired and begin to fall asleep I am at times bombarded with space debris telepathy and sometimes-deliberate attacks of violent image telepathy from other sick violent people. On occasion when I am very tired, very sick, or have a migraine headache my mind is weak against telepathic images with my eyes closed as I am preparing for sleep. My eyes are closed during the flooding of my conscious by these unwanted telepathic images. With my eyes open I do receive occasional telepathic image attacks but normally these are very easy to repel if violent or unwanted. These violent telepathic images are generally attacks from violent people who wish to hurt or control me, or simply test my skills of telepathy against theirs.

All the images sent to me from other people in my life have always been sent to the interior of my conscious mind; I never as yet received an outside projection from other people projected into the outside world. When I was driving semi-truck cross-country and through large cities in the United States a lot of people were familiar with my telepathy and wished to test me with their own telepathic skills. Just like the gunslinger of the Wild West I am always called out for a gunfight to test my telepathic skills against their telepathy abilities. Some people get lucky now and then with their Flip images attacking me while my eyes are open but these image attacks only happen occasionally and as I said before and they are very easy to repel. However with my eyes shut I am vulnerable when tired to attacks of unwanted telepathic images by other people.

Please make note of the fact that if I wanted to share telepathic images with a person with my eyes closed there would be no problem if there was co-operation, mutual trust and no violence involved.

When I first started to do image Flipping I observed that a lot of the people preferred violence in their telepathy so I realized right away that there would be a problem down the line with constant violent attacks of telepathy against me. Right from the beginning I tried to train my mind to repel these violent thoughts by practicing the void technique and thank goodness I did.

If unwanted thoughts are flowing into your conscious mind then the **total void technique** of meditation is one of the ways to learn to control these intrusive thoughts. This void technique is concentrating with your eyes closed seeking to empty your internal conscious gallery of all light, images, and thoughts of any kind. You want to see only "void". Void is not black, black is a saturated color and very hard to totally attain. The void will be hard to describe because we never concentrate on void so there is no color name for void. It may appear gray black; you should name the color void or any other name you so desire to help you go there in your mind. You may see very small dots of light color such as gray or gray brown with your eyes closed and these are simple imperfections on your retina that the previous viewed light has burned a bit and should just be ignored for void meditation.

All this concentrating on void and turning away all conscious thoughts is difficult to attain in the beginning but as you work at it you will learn to take control of your conscious mind. Progress will be slow but you should begin to have some control after practicing this meditation technique for 10 -15 minutes per day for about three months time. After a year you will notice definite **control** and more importantly no fear of some thoughts that you cannot control at times. You could increase your time to 30 minutes a day if you so desire this only a matter of convenience if you have the time. This daily meditation schedule sounds rigorous but it is not, it is a simple daily routine to be established and then time flies by and progress is realized.

Meditation may also be accomplished with the eyes shut concentrating on a **slightly illuminated focal point in the dark of your interior conscious mind.** A person may also focus on breathing; maybe try **breathing through your hands** feeling the airflow through your hands with a type of imaginary telepathy. Before I practiced the void technique I concentrated on the illusion of breathing through my hands and this proved to be a good concentration exercise for stress relief.

A person may try to produce **colors or simple geometric shapes** while concentrating with your eyes closed. These shapes may have color contrast or the much easier to do dark shapes on a dark background and if so desired given illumination as an object in the interior galleries of your conscious mind as you meditate with your eyes shut.

A variation of meditation may be **susurrations of the wind** providing a soothing and relaxing flow of sound and touch telepathy as you Flip in harmony with nature's wind. You simply repeat nice things in your mind that you project with sound telepathy slightly outward with moderate to strong winds passing over your ears. Try to be in harmony with the sound of the wind and the feel of the wind touching your face **synchronizing both the sound and touch of the wind with the push out of your conscious thoughts using telepathy.** You may also imagine pushing bad thoughts out into the wind's feel and sound providing catharsis resulting in stress relief.

It is also possible to **meditate to music** and push your bad thoughts out of your conscious mind into the beat of the music with sound Flip. This pushing of your bad thoughts into the music with sound Flip will empty your mind of stress and other poison thoughts.

People meditating together focusing on a single sound or music playing could create an ambiance of beautiful feelings with telepathy summation emotions that are pushed out and amplified through the group's focused synchronization on this sound.

Summation Group

All sensory capacities and telepathy methods described in this book may be entered into a summation group topic. These summation groups may occur formally requiring a lot of formal preparation or may simply be a chance encounter with relative strangers in a public place. Concentrated formal group summation of course will be more intense and productive. All the senses, emotion, touching, smelling, hearing, tasting, and seeing all may be enhanced and amplified with summation group Flip by pulling more psychic energy together for increased thought power. Sound Flip clapping the word Love in church, Flipping the touch and sound of the wind on your face in meditation, the aroma of flowers in a field, listening to an orchestra playing music, sharing a large dinner feast with many people or watching a sunset on the ocean all may be group summated with Flip and enhanced. Awareness is increased with telepathy and group summation telepathy helps to increase this awareness even more.

Casual Group Summation

When mental telepathy is running and perceived by a group of people in close proximity to each other, their short term and long term memories automatically add related pieces to the telepathy concepts that are happening all around them. **This automatic piecing of information from other people during telepathy helps build concepts for this relative group and also helps this particular group in remembering information and following through on set job tasks.**

The offices of big successful business along with various production factories will begin to incorporate problem solving through mental telepathy summation and this will take place in a passive informal manner once the office personnel have been taught formal synchronized Flip. Once taught formal telepathy; then passive telepathy should occur naturally on its own.

I have done a large number of mental exercises with people using passive group telepathy summation and this seems to help members of a group in remembering short term memory tasks, which will reduce the number of mistakes in the office or factory. The passive telepathy here indicates no formal construction of stated goals or mandatory synchronization of a particular thought, telepathy occurring as random synchronization, which provides help with the various routine job tasks throughout the office work day.

The sharing of thoughts with telepathy gives a feeling of harmony to the originator's mind and reinforces the concept as a good one or a bad one. If during casual summation telepathy the originator of a thought senses a positive reinforcement then this will give confidence to continue building this idea. Just the sharing of a thought with another person gives the human mind great comfort from communicating with another human being and also supplies a reward of feelings similar to that of a pat on the back for correct thinking. This telepathy exchange creates a cozy ambiance for increased productivity and as mentioned before helps in remembering casual job tasks.

One technique for the work area would be to play music that is soothing and contains a distinctive rhythm that makes it easy to push out mental telepathy on a casual basis occasionally throughout the day at random by employees but not necessary all the time. After a month of telepathy training has been accomplished with a distinctive beat of music, I think any type of music can then be substituted and played at any volume to serve as an auxiliary helper and achieve passive telepathy summation in the office. The music may then serve to continue to passively synchronize all minds in the office for group summation once the telepathy instruction has been learned. After the group practices telepathy for a couple of months with music, the music may be discontinued if wished.

Group Flip summation requires cooperation and trust from the other people working in the office area that enables an individual to open his or her mind to others. In order for people to open their minds and lower protective ***conscious shields*** in the factory or office the surrounding environment must be free of all violent thinking. The less thinking there is of violent thoughts among the workers, the more open to telepathy and more productive the factory or office will be. The work area should not be a place where hateful people are allowed to practice their intrusive thought attacks. People of a hateful nature will not be welcome in the work arena of co-operative business in the near future. Hateful personalities will break this trust and be disruptive to intelligent concentration not allowing summation of minds to occur. Many people will also become aware of ethics and sensitivity of other people through the practicing of telepathy with trust, thus improving the ambiance of the work or office place.

Formal Concentration Summation Telepathy

Concentrated and more serious summation work will need a 72 hour cleansing of the group's short term memory of Deviant Sex, Violence, and other guilt producing data prior to the forming of the summation group. Normal everyday casual telepathy summation will not need so formal and stringent cleansing of the short term memory.

All this mental cleaning enhances the job of working with summation image Flip and holding images in place by reducing short term memory interference preventing the group from needing to siphon off energy to push this unwanted interference away and reducing job concentration. This formal group summating will enable them to seek solutions such as pieces of the DNA molecule being assembled and examined by scientists; or possible the creation and assembly of the architecture of a building constructed during this summation groups' use of image Flip.

Not only does telepathy produce shared images, it also downloads and connects memories for future reference. Formal Telepathy work with physical senses and word concepts may also be concentrated on. In addition resources beyond our wildest dreams are opened with telepathy for problem solving on a 24-hour basis through the universal mind.

Formal Group Summation Requirements

1 - Honesty and Trust for lowering of conscious protective shielding

2 - Ability to Concentrate

3 - Quiet comfortable area

4 - Voluntary co-operation of all participants

5 - Able to focus on a physical sense, object, place, word concept, field of color or a dark void free of any illumination.

6 - Proper Vocabulary of the working summation topic.

7 - No Violent Thoughts

8 - Good knowledge of what the proper image, feeling, or other sensing that is expected to occur

within the group's summation project.

9 - Serious work will need 72 hour cleansing of short term memory.

The term ***Collective Conscious*** has just become true with the increased practice of Flip in the world. Collective Consciousness is Summation Telepathy of a current shared thought when synchronized and then permanently contained in the Universal Mind.

Collective Conscience is the morals model set forth by majority thinking used for thought comparison concerning correctness in human rights and treatment stored in living human memories also contained in the Universal Mind or Universal Memory.

Primitive example of group summation by animals?

While driving a motorcycle in Costa Rica in one of the Caribbean Ocean National Parks a group of maybe 10 to 20 Howling Monkeys became irritated by the sound of my motorcycle passing by them on the dirt road in front of their group sitting in mango trees and they voiced their disgust by howling. The sound shock of these monkeys howling in unison was not from the planet earth. The sound was beyond awesome and indescribably loud. I thought that I was being buzzed overhead by a 747 jet airplane landing at the airport. I said to myself that positively there was a 747 jet airplane overhead blasting those big jet engines above my head. I was flown around Europe while in the military by jets and in my travels in civilian life I have also flown in quite a few 747 jet airplanes to Costa Rica, and I swear by the God's that this noise I was hearing was a 747 and it had to be only 200 meters or less landing above my head and incredibly loud.

So there I am in the jungle along the ocean looking up for this 747 overhead when in reality there is not an airport for 200 miles that could accommodate a 747, but Oh my gosh it had to be there. It was not a 747 but rather a troop of monkeys! The Howling Monkeys were in perfect harmony and had made this unbelievable shocking noise. As I drove by the monkeys this intense sound continued for a duration of about 30 seconds then it died down. I drove my motorcycle maybe 2 kilometers past the monkeys where I stopped, looked around and tried to figure out what had happened. I said to myself that somebody must have some super loud speakers out here in this jungle and playing some kind of joke on me, something I myself might pull. I then said to myself, is that outrageous sound really those monkeys? So I turned around and passed in front of the monkeys once again. To my surprise the monkeys did it again but only about 50% as loud as the first time but still a fantastic volume. To this day I don't know for sure if the monkeys used my telepathic mind for a medium to increase their volume or it was their perfect resonance resulting in fantastic volume or maybe all the above. I would like to think that this was summation telepathy by me and the monkeys and wow was it an incredible sound to behold not from planet earth. And I said animals are not capable of telepathy, maybe I'm not totally correct in stating that.

Summation Telepathy Interference from the Short Term Memory

Interference coming from the **short term memory is generally the most powerful concepts reproduced and returned as latent power thoughts back into the conscious for a second time after formerly being cleared from the conscious**. During a planned summation group of telepathy this interference that is shooting back out of the short term memory will shut down group concentration especially when using image summation projections.

It also seems to take 30 seconds or more for the conscious to ignore a thought that has appeared in the conscious and is now discarded into the ***pre-conscious***. Before this 30 second time period is up the thought is still partially perceived in the pre-conscious and tries to reappear in the conscious again now for the second time.

The conscious must make an effort to ward off all thoughts not pertinent to a telepathy summation work topic that are coming from the short-term memory and pre-conscious. An extended time period free from non-pertinent interference must be maintained for the summation group to continue concentrating on its chosen topic that they are currently working on.

A healthy conscious normally repels all previous viewed thoughts. On occasion a strikingly powerful thought will return again into the conscious unable to be repelled because the striking nature of the thought made its energy too powerful: such as magnificent color, size, movement, speed, or high emotion attached to the previously discarded concept.

Most recently seen images which are filed in the **72 hour short term memory** are some of the most frequent thought interference cropping up in a group practicing summation telepathy. **As said before, a group of people who is expecting to perform an agreed neural network would have to cleanse their mind of violence, sexual explicit scenes, and possible other shocking images for 72**

hours prior to their summation work. These types of thoughts possess a lot of power to break into the conscious again from the short term memory and will instantly ruin a mental telepathy summation group when the minds of the group become afraid or distracted from internal violence or guilt stemming from the short term memories high energy thoughts.

The conscious mind has low resistance to violent attacks when its conscious shields are lowered in shared telepathy summation. The lowering of all protective barriers is a primary requirement for the sharing of thoughts when problem solving in a formal summation telepathy group. It is possible that the agreed people in a neural network can work together to resist and drive back violent or other destructive thoughts thus maintaining good telepathy summation concentration as they push away outside non-pertinent intrusive thoughts. With all conscious shielding lowered by the people in the summation group consideration must be taken for the immediate surrounding area of the summation ring that is practicing telepathy. With all the conscious shielding lowered the group's sensitivity will drastically increase and the shock of violence from other violent people outside the group ring will be strong if in close proximity to the summation group or family in the home; this violent interference will result in the contamination of the group's concentrated topic and causing temporary anxiety.

Causal telepathy summation in church praying or singing, watching a sunset together in a group, having a group dinner etc., does not have to have a lot of intensity of concentration for summation amplification to occur. Being aware of the types of distractions that can contaminate subject matter that reduce the power of the group while in summation telepathy will increase spontaneous summation pertaining to casual summation Flip, especially always trying to repel violence.

Downloading Violence

A large quantity of violence should not be downloaded into the mind over a short time because of the fact that down the road **violence will constantly leak out of the memories through mental telepathy and offend people**. It may be considered unethical in the near future to allow the downloading of violent thoughts to a child from the media or books. Downloading violence could lead to the child being ostracized because he or she was taught violence and is considered by others as too offensive in a non-violent group of children going into the future. All the forms of telepathy transmit stored memory violence to public awareness, many times unintentionally.

The Media is by far the most important contributing factor to downloading violence into the short term and long term memories through the reading of violent novels, viewing violent movies, television news, newspapers, magazines, and the playing of violent video games.

Environmental live violence in nature such as the graphic killing of one animal against another in the wild for survival is a natural viewing occurrence. These things we witness quite commonly from the cat and mouse murder to humans slaughtering cattle for hamburgers. Wind storms, fires, earthquakes, volcanoes, and floods are events of nature characterized by traumatic destruction of human life that results in the viewing and downloading of violence.

Human Pain - Thoughts of pain are a natural thing to ponder in the course of a day and are a form of violence to the human mind that will interfere with all telepathy. Many things represent human pain and violence such as the birthing process of the human fetus. The violent pain experienced by the birthing mother and the baby presented to the world as a bloody mess, and the tearing away of the placenta from the uterine wall with still more blood are forms of natural occurring human violence. Many fathers present in the delivery room have witnessed this traumatic scene.

Human manual labor always results in pain and very slight injuries to the body such as a simple callous of the hands or sore muscles and even calluses from normal walking. The brain also imagines various hurt and pain scenarios for protection. The mind projects images of possible sequences that may occur in the future such as avoiding stepping off a cliff, getting bitten by wild animals or even the imagined action of getting hit crossing a busy street in traffic, which is necessary for the protection of the person. Even sex is sometimes viewed as a violent act. Pain and violence will constantly be present downloading into the memories for recall and preventing telepathy by violent interference later.

It might not be required to totally eliminate the downloading of violence for the human mind; rather regulate the amount of inputted violence that we receive over a time period especially the 72 hour period that is the extent of the short term memory.

If violence is a natural and unavoidable given for the functioning of the human life, then we will need to accept and regulate it as it looks as though violence will always be straying through our minds. **This downloaded violence must be controlled and managed thus requiring a little concentration to push it away from the conscious focus from time to time.**

Controlling the short term memory's intake of violence over 72 hour period may be one of the keys to controlling criminal violence in society.

Emotion Telepathy

A person is able to project good emotional feelings out of their mind through mental telepathy with a light concentrated push out effort. People who work at projecting loving feelings with telepathy out into their household create a cozy ambiance well worth the effort. I think that this emotion telepathy push out should be fairly easy to do with family members who are familiar with each others' thinking. All people in the household should be on the same telepathy channel so to speak and thus will have complete trust with one another for opening of all consciouses by the lowering of the conscious shielding that normally is in place for protection from the harms of society.

Just think nice thoughts and concentrate on pushing them out of your conscious mind into the environment of the home. A parent may practice pushing the word love out from their conscious mind into the home environment. Over a period of time say approximately six months you will begin to need less effort to push these good emotional feelings of love out of your interior mind and into your home. A mother or other family member may also sound Flip the word love into music playing from the radio or other source in the home on a daily basis randomly.

Everybody picks up on emotional mental telepathy but when it comes to the measurement of proficiency for the reception all people vary here on their degree of recognition of these emotion telepathy transmissions. Still a lot of people are actually quite good at picking up on emotional projected feelings. In the home around family members whose minds are well known along with trust, emotional telepathy should be easier to perceive. In creating an emotional projected ambiance in and around the household the outside world and its Machiavellian problems seem far away. It takes only a small amount of effort to project this surround ambiance but with practice I know a person would learn to accomplish this mental task with very little energy drain and in time it would become an automatic process.

It would be nice if a community was able to put forth the effort to project emotional mental telepathy throughout the city with good thoughts; a far out concept but easy to do with practice.

Summation Emotion Flip - A crowd of people sharing joint thoughts or goals should quite easily increase the power of their emotional feelings through summation Flip. One example of this type of behavior would be a church worship. Some people in this church group may be weak with mental telepathy, some strong, all flowing together amplifying their experience of worship. This group summation telepathy in church creates an ambiance around them of strong-shared emotions through the practiced concentration of mental telepathy pushed out into the group; this may take 1 or 2 meetings but this is easily accomplished. Hand clapping could be used in conjunction with emotions by pushing emotions into the rhythm and sound of the hand clapping.

The trick here is learning to trust other people in the summation group and have no violent thinking. This trusting atmosphere gives confidence in one another enabling the mind to lower its shields of conscious protection for co-operation in thought enhancement and amplification within the group summation. The church service is one place where this trust and co-operation should all be taking place automatically; and with a little mental concentration push out the telepathy will enhance the church service and their goals or any other group meeting along with creating an emotional ambiance. The awareness among group members that telepathy is real and functions to amplify emotions will be enough to get the telepathy going in the group.

From all my practical experience of thousands of Flips with emotional mental telepathy I would have to definitely **declare emotion the 6th sense**. When Flip symbols are transmitted such as a word with sound Flip, emotions may or may not be attached. When emotions are attached to the word sounds Flipped, the emotions that have been purposely attached to the telepathy are picked up by all. Testing for these emotions was done by Flipping the exact same word sounds every time; and then adding emotions to the Flip projection and feedback occurring in the form of vocalizations of exactly which emotion was attempted such as sad, happy or love when attached. When emotions are not attached to the Flip projection, no emotions are reported back.

This is why emotion has to be the 6th sense because feelings are always sensed when transmitted with Flip and vocalized back. One of the examples that I used to validate emotions was an image of a newborn baby or simply the word sound baby, sometimes attaching happy emotions and sometimes crying sad and both were always differentiated and reported back with vocals.

A person should try to always think nice thoughts especially when around family and friends because through the everyday exercise of telepathy some thoughts will begin to leak out of your mind without the effort of the conscious push out. Flip could easily leak out into your foot talking or as you are washing the dishes through sound Flip using the running water's sound. This leaking out of thought transference while washing dishes sounds silly but it will happen quite frequently. **There will naturally be a few times that bad things will come out of your mind with telepathy and a person should try to restrain these bad thoughts around family and friends. The same holds true for your significant other who should not take all bad Flips to heart, we are not perfect beings as of yet.** Many bad things with be projected accidentally with Flip telepathy but not meant as intentional hurt and should be ignored unless the frequency becomes great.

Mental telepathy **amplifies silliness along with violence** and these emotions have to be reduced as telepathy skills and age increase. If not corrected this amplification of these emotions will irritate and punish other people and more importantly one's self. More thought control is required as a person practices telepathy and grows older requiring self actualization of emotions while practicing telepathy.

Things to consider as you practice your Flip skills

1- **Writing Sarcasm hurts** a person's feelings.

2- **Speaking Sarcasm hurts** people's feelings.

3- **Now for the first time with the new practice of mental telepathy projection**, **emotional thoughts of a hurting nature although not vocalized, do harm in other people's conscious mind producing psychological harm especially if the originator continues to dwell upon this particular bad thought.** Flipping strong correct emotional thinking should foster a strong hard foundation for future development of intelligence in the family home with a conscience memory instilled over time with moral correctness.

Future generations must be able to handle more powerful emotions that will come about through awareness and amplification accomplished by telepathy.

As emotions become more intense with Flip added we must be careful when choosing our friends and beware of our acquaintances or we may all die of a broken heart.

Telepathy as a Teaching Aid and Help for the Mentally Handicapped

<u>Foot Talking</u> is one telepathy method that has proven to be a great way to teach young children to learn to read. Children can walk and spell three and four letter words with their feet one letter per step with foot talking telepathy. Animals may be painted on the sidewalk and when the children encounter them they may spell the animal such as the word **c-o-w** with telepathy footsteps or in conjunction with regular vocal repetition. In addition simple **A-B-C's** may be spelled out walking with foot talking telepathy steps.

I have a program that uses <u>ten symbols</u> for preschoolers to learn to spell. I use, dog, cat, pig, cow, sun, star, car, ball, fish, and bee for symbols to teach children to read. Another method is to put the words printed under the images on a place mat and on the back of the place mat printing only the word itself, alternating sides of the place mat at different meals. You then set these place mats on the dinner table for children to view. We need to use only ten symbols in the beginning, this makes it easier to facilitate the children's reading skill by repetition. Once these ten symbols have been mastered we can then move on to other symbols for the pre-schooler to learn.

<u>Bouncing Ball Sound Telepathy</u> may be a tool that works for some children helping recite their A-B-C's or spelling words. Form a word in your mind and then simply bounce a rubber ball and push a syllable of word or a single letter of this word silently from your mind into the ball as it makes the physical contact with the ground. When the rubber ball contacts a hard surface it simultaneously emits a perfect smacking sound great for inserting a syllable or letter of word with sound telepathy or simply a letter of the alphabet while at play. So you are synchronizing the combination of the ball's point of sight physical contact with the ground along with the sound of the ball and then pushing one syllable of word from your mind into these two synchronized points with silent telepathy from your conscious mind; very, very easy to do.

Mental mathematics is something we normally all do in our heads with mental image projection. With a little more concentrated effort and daily practice, improved and clearer internal mental images pushed out or internalized in the **conscious gallery** should become easier with practice and facilitate the inner blackboard for problem solving. Teaching children early in school internal conscious imaging for problem solving or projected telepathy images out on to a small white marker board at the front of the classroom would be great. This sounds a little far-fetched but I think this could easily be accomplished and would be good for the children to learn telepathy image projections, both internally and to the outside environment on this white marker board for mathematics.

The teacher or other speakers naturally will distract the student's projections if students are looking at them. For this reason the white marker board or screen should be above the teacher's head and slightly above the blackboard to avoid viewing the teacher along with his or her distractions when projections are necessary. I tend to think an elevated white board with the students imagining to project black lettering on this white board is best, adding and subtracting simple math problems there. A black board that an individual imagines projecting white writing also works well and the ordinary classroom blackboard may suffice if necessary.

Foot talking and sound telepathy are beginning to take hold in this world from the conception of the fetus. Pregnant mothers practicing foot talking while walking around synchronizing words with their feet along with sound telepathy while listening to music may possible teach her fetus mental telepathy passively while the fetus is growing in her womb.

The pregnant mother may also practice telepathy in a more concentrated and synchronized way such as synchronizing her own heartbeat with Flip to the fetus and possible brief moments when the fetus moves or kicks. Another method for teaching the fetus is to gently tap or massage the pregnant mother's abdomen with the mother's hand or the father's hand while at the same time synchronizing words with sound Flip or touching vibration Flip. This helps to facilitate the area of the brain for future use of mental telepathy when language skills appear.

New Born Facilitated Pathway Branching - Mother's who practice mental telepathy while pregnant may also benefit their fetus if it is born mentally handicapped. Slow children will have alternate neural pathways already facilitated a little by telepathy for a contingency available to help jump start communication when language skills appear.

It is better to facilitate branching of neural pathways by starting stimulus of the newborn in the crib with music and color mobiles right through infancy. It is possible that intelligent pathways are achieved through stimulation and produce more neural branching allowing them more spatial room for neuron thinking in the infinite mind.

If a neural pathway does not branch soon enough in childhood it is open for more potential destruction along its course later in life. The more neural branches facilitated in a young child's mind the more optional repair lines may be available for working around a damage area in the brain using psychic energy if damage should develop in the future. Telepathy may help by using psychic energy to connect broken routes in conjunction with normal energy paths to continue moving the thought through the neural system into the memories and the conscious mind. **Psychic energy is a given found everywhere in the universe in abundance and the key to harnessing this free psychic energy for thought transference is the synchronization of this psychic energy.**

Telepathy may reroute nerve signals around damaged areas of the brain with Flip by the forming of countless variable connections of neural pathways similar to the analogy of 1 billion miles of extension cord however telepathy will transverse this great distance instantaneously making this vast rerouting unimportant.

I was sitting at a bus stop in Costa Rica, Central America waiting with a mother and her baby for the bus to come. I watched the Mother playing patty cake with her 3 month old child teaching thought transference to the baby through the slapping of the baby's hand in her hand, an awesome sight. I invented this sound Flip stuff but when I saw this mother doing sound Flip and touching her baby's hands in a game of patty cake I was truly impressed. The telepathy games that mothers play with their children who they have around them all the time will probably never cease to amaze me. Awesome!

Theories of Psychic Energy Restoring Brain Damaged Pathways

The following are 2 different ways that telepathy may travel around weak or dead areas of the brain. Be aware that restoring nerve pathways may be using these following two theories or more all at the same time to restore proper function of thought conductivity again to the conscious.

Circumvent Problem Areas by Psychic Energy

Theory 1 Circumventing damaged points and reconnecting them to working neural lines by using synchronized psychic energy, which looks for a route to the conscious rerouting itself through an infinite number of extensions to get to the conscious. The analogy of a billion miles of extension cords connected together by psychic energy enabling the thought to finally be viewed in the conscious now as psychic energy traverses this billion miles of extension cords instantly.

Piggybacking Senses

Theory 2 It is possible to teach people to piggyback a non-working sensory system onto one that is a working sensory system by synchronizing a normal psychic energy thought with bio-chemical energy from another system thereby completing sensory perception in the conscious. An example of piggybacking another working sense system here would be a thought attached by telepathy to the skeletal nerve pathway through the practice of **foot talking** or **jogging vibrations.** This will reroute the synchronized psychic energy thought around the broken or weak connections in the thinking neural pathway through the network of the synchronization of the skeletal muscle neural systems, which synchronizes the thought with the skeletal muscle's bio-chemical energies accomplishing summation of energies enabling the thought to now reach the conscious focus.

This use of an alternate system's energy keeps the normal conscious thought processes rolling along in a continuous train of thought by synchronizing psychic energy thoughts with alternate physical bio-chemical energies then pushing this thought to the conscious. This however is of course slower in relation to the speed of the foot talking synchronization and its time allowed for stepping.

In addition my hearing sense is greatly aided by observing with my eyes something with movement and adding synchronized telepathy that I have named the Illusion of Sound, explained page 115.

Motivation for Teaching Handicapped

I have read quite a lot of material along with viewing many films, and received a lot of letters from people working with mentally handicapped children and they all report on how hard they work to improve their child's mental condition. **A person may not be proficient in thought transference techniques but when working with your own child you have a *higher motivation level* providing added confidence in your telepathy skills for helping your child.**

I will not give any parent false hope and I will not lie to you about telepathy to make it sound great; telepathy is truly great. There are so many lies and deception in the psychic business that it is hard to take any of this mental telepathy seriously. However, I am here to tell you there is solid hope with this telepathy and this may be the ticket to helping your child. Keep at it with a positive attitude and you are going to improve your child's condition with one of these telepathy techniques.

Teaching Mentally Handicapped
Foot Talking

Foot talking has proven to be one way for insane people to communicate words with their feet one syllable of word per step at a time. I am talking about people here who cannot put together one sentence of thought that makes any sense and believe me there is a lot of people like this tucked away in our society. **The foot talking is slow but for the first time in who knows how long these insane people make sense by foot talking.** These particular insane people just loved to talk with their feet and I have watched the whole floor of the mental ward at the Veteran's Military Hospital in Los Angeles, California talk all day long from sun up to sun down with their feet; these insane people could not get enough of this foot talking. These insane people know they are making sense with foot talking and enjoy it immensely.

We need to take note here that these people who I have observed were declared insane by many psychiatrists, however earlier in their life they were not insane and they were capable of normal comprehension and vocal expression. In their later life these people became insane from physical damage to their brain. These insane people all served in the military when they were younger and at that time were considered normal mentally.

Taciturn Children

Flip is non-offensive to the human psyche and I believe that some children that dislike normal vocal sounds can benefit from teachers possessing telepathic skills. Taciturn children may adapt to mental telepathy communication more readily than normal talking; telepathy being an independent type of language of its own and also being non-offensive to the mentally handicapped. All this telepathy does not have to replace normal talking but rather to help facilitate normal talking. This telepathy goes directly into the conscious mind and then proceeds to slowly encode language sounds into the short term and then long term memories; doing all this while being non-offensive to the handicapped child's mind.

Teachers of mentally handicapped children or parents should remember that many forms of telepathy can be mouthed or **"Lip Synched"** without vocal sound to help form words more clearly in your mind and then transmit these words outward from the conscious mind with telepathy. Normal voice might always be better with some mentally handicapped people and telepathy just an auxiliary helper by synchronizing the spoken words while lip synchronizing. The sound of your spoken word may be sound Flipped along with the motion Flip all by listening intently and lip synchronizing.

Sound Telepathy - A good method for teaching taciturn children is sound Flip shown in the following examples.

Instructing children to play with an air hose equipped with an on/off push button nozzle is one way to play and learn with sound telepathy. The child can spray air having fun and learning to communicate with the world by sound telepathy that also facilitates communication for normal speaking in the brain. **This spraying of air has a precise sound to it that is great for repeating words with sound Flip** that are first spoken by the teacher. I would suggest safety glasses for the children while spraying the air nozzle to prevent eye irritation if sprayed too close to the eyes.

I once had a temporary job for a month working in a factory that manufactured small metal fittings for hydraulic hoses. The parts needed to be cleaned by oil and then two of us (myself and my friend) sprayed the oil off with an air hose, 6 hours a day, five days a week. My partner loved to talk with his air gun as he was spraying the oil off the small metal fittings so I naturally joined in conversing with my air hose also. My friend and I carried on a conversation for 6 hours a day with sound Flip and the air guns really did not offend our minds while we continually did this sound Flip throughout the day while at work. The air hoses have a precise sound that is easy and great fun.

Another good technique to use for sound Flip would be a type of sound producing video game. A taciturn child could play a video game with sound such as a car driving game for sound telepathy learning. The sound telepathy is very easy to do and the computer game's sound type can be adjusted to make the sound Flip easy for the taciturn child to perform. When the child accomplishes sound telepathy he or she will be rewarded with extended time on the game or any other reward by the teacher. **If the teacher is touching the video game in any way, he or she may instruct the taciturn pupil in sound Flip by touching the game and then Flipping word concepts with lip synchronization for the child to hear and try to duplicate on their own with telepathy. Many game controllers now have a vibration option that may also be used for telepathy synchronization.**

Along this same line of thought is to use a small hand held speaking computer for teaching. I can't say enough about these little computers that talk words. Children as young as one year old love playing with these speaking computers and may learn to speak words of their own using one. Again, telepathy may be used in conjunction with the speaking computer to **help in language acquisition by overlapping the computer's sound of the word with sound Flip aided with lip synchronization; this knowledge will then penetrate deep into the memories for future retrieval.**

The small hand held computer may also produce a simple type of sound that is easy to transmit sound telepathy with. In this manner the speaking word hand held computer may alternate words spoken followed by a sound void of spoken words that is conducive for sound Flipping only if desired.

A teacher could use a drum for sound Flip work holding the hand of the handicapped person as they both strike the drum. This drumming not only provides sound, but also touching (vibration with percussion), and synchronization with sight or light as the drum is contacted. Simply Flip one syllable of word with one strike of the drum. Slow children may also be able to talk or spell words with musical notes such as using a xylophone, piano, guitar or perhaps a beat of a drum with sound telepathy.

Normally a conscious thought is brought forward and held in focus in the conscious gallery by the brain's physical bio-chemical electrical energy that is used to synchronize and capture a thought. Mentally handicapped children sometimes cannot capture or concentrate on a concept in their conscious mind. **A group performing telepathy summation in a classroom can hold a thought in the handicapped child's conscious gallery for them by first capturing the thought normally in the group's mind then transferring the thought into the conscious of the handicapped person's mind with telepathy.** This will enable the handicapped person's conscious memory to hold a telepathic thought long enough to begin to facilitate the thought to the short term and long term memories for retrieval in the future. Teaching handicapped people by using Flip summation in the classroom will also help provide recognition of all concepts by adding pieces for completion and highlighting some thoughts for the taciturn person's conscious.

So we now know that if the needed physical energy is lacking for thought capture in the handicapped person's brain a summation group may put a thought into the handicapped person's conscious with telepathy.

If the summation telepathy methods do not speed up the learning process for speaking language, **telepathy will definitely down the line and for the rest of their lives enable handicapped children's long term memory to relate to the correct pronunciation of the word** that will be entered into the long term memory through telepathy. The speech of the handicapped person will improve with clarity for their total life as they match the sound of their voice with the correct memory imprints from summation telepathy in the classroom previously.

Sound telepathy can be used to help children who are slow to talk by priming their communication area of the brain and **molding their voice with summation Flip to match the correct sounding word**.

<u>Bouncing Ball Sound Telepathy</u> as mentioned before may be used as a tool that works for some taciturn children. Forming a word in your mind and then simply bouncing a rubber ball and pushing a syllable of this word silently from your mind into the rubber ball as it makes contact with the ground. When the ball contacts a hard surface it simultaneously emits a perfect smacking sound great for inserting a syllable of word with sound telepathy. So you are capable of synchronizing the combination of the ball's point of sight contact as it contacts the ground along with the sound of the rubber ball and then pushing one syllable of word from your mind into these two synchronized points with silent telepathy from your conscious mind.

I have noticed that a lot of paranoid schizophrenics and other mentally handicapped people are not in the least bit afraid of mental telepathy; rather they seem to enjoy it as much as the next person and normally a lot more.

When I first noticed that mentally handicapped people were not afraid of mental telepathy I was very surprised because in the beginning I thought that Flip would hurt their mind and they would "freak out" by undermining their sense of reality.

I worked as a day laborer on a temporary job with a mentally handicapped person all day long washing chemical buckets out and the man hated to talk vocally to me yet he talked with the water hose using sound telepathy for the whole eight hours non-stop. I tried to start a conversation with common vocals and the man got extremely upset with me.

This man said I talked too much and then he went right back to talking with the water hose using sound telepathy conversing with this type of telepathy the entire 8 hours to me. **Wow!** I could not believe it but I later witnessed this type of behavior many times with sound telepathy and foot talking communication occurring with the mentally handicapped.

<u>It seems the physical sound of a device or machine when accompanied with telepathy does not offend a mentally handicapped person's mind as normal vocals sometimes do</u>. I have observed perhaps 50 random observations of paranoid schizophrenics of which none of them were afraid of telepathy and perhaps the total truth remains to be seen but this gives a ray of hope for aiding the mentally handicapped as they show no fear or aversion to this mental telepathy.

Taciturn or other young mentally handicapped children can also be taught foot talking that would help bring more neural pathways into play and possible start facilitation of communication skills in the brain and aid in language skills.

<u>Mute</u> - Some mute people for whatever the reason are not able to talk normally but are capable of producing guttural sounds from deep in their throat. These primitive guttural sounds can be used for communicating with sound Flip very easily. **A small sound-producing device may also be carried and used for sound telepathy with ease if the person is mute.** There are many digital electronic sound producing devices on the market that could easily hang on a necklace or possible clip on your wrist or belt for your sound Flip communication of thought if vocal sounds are not present.

I was attending a carnival in Costa Rica and a man working in one of the fair's booths could not speak but could easily make guttural sounds. I taught the man sound Flip in about two minute's time. In two minutes time this man's life of 35 years was instantly changed as he now had a nice way to communicate with people and friends with sound Flip. Highly sensational but every person who reads this page is capable of teaching this minor miracle to a mute person.

Autistic Children - If some form of language skill is available and presently working in the autistic child's mind they may benefit from practicing telepathy. When using telepathy with an autistic child, physical conscious sense input from the external world sometimes confuses the child's conscious mind, which interferes with teaching concepts. The "Pure Form of Telepathy" is heard in the conscious gallery of the autistic child without the complication of physical sound that causes confusion. If desired the teaching to the autistic person can be void of the distraction of a speaking person making offensive sounds by using the fore mentioned telepathy technique of pure telepathy.

A teenager from India by the name of Tito Mukhopadhyay has given invaluable data about the problems of autistic people's inabilities to focus and concentrate on a single concept. **Tito has pointed out that it is only possible for him to focus on one sense at a time; "so he can feel or hear, but not both and switching from one to the other is a great effort.** Tito is a good writer and explains his condition to others through his writings. Tito says the reason for selecting a single sense at a time is to keep the flood of visual and sound distortions apart from his single concept he is focused on. Flip projection is kind of the same way, being that the more senses are involved, the more complicated telepathy becomes.

Telepathy projection also possesses the possibility to bypass all complex physical functions and transmit an idea directly into the conscious gallery for memorization and encoding. This may be projected with one simple physical sense thereby producing less confusion in the conscious gallery of the autistic person through "Pure" telepathy. Strobe light telepathy may also be beneficial to autistic children.

Teaching the Deaf to Hear

Piggyback Senses- As mentioned before it is possible to teach people to piggyback a non-working physical sensory system onto one that is a working physical sensory system by adding telepathy; thereby completing sensory perception in the conscious by adding this working sense with synchronized psychic energy. **My hearing sense is greatly aided by observing with my eyes something with movement and adding telepathy.** For example; if I observe a spider or gecko lizard crawling I seem to hear the legs each stepping clearly through my practicing of telepathy and in turn people around me for as far as one hundred meters or more can hear the creature's amplified stepping through me also. This might be a real telepathy sense transmission or a transmitted illusion by the use of telepathy. **If this is an illusion by telepathy, this illusion can still create the sense of hearing that in essence is the same as the real thing to the senses of the internal human mind.** Mind to mind telepathy never has to obey physical law because we are using the internal mind's psychic energy and not physical energy for the carrying of thought.

Illusion of Sound Technique for Deaf People- First a deaf person needs to have a type of sound imprinted in his or her memories. This is done by telepathy of another person who already has this particular sound recorded in their normal hearing memories. This could be accomplished by a single teacher or a group of people agreeing on transmitting one specific sound by telepathy into the deaf person or class of deaf peoples' memories. This telepathy sound goes deep into the memories and is filed for future use by the deaf person. This chosen **telepathic sound is filed into the memories of the deaf person and then it is retrieved when necessary from the deaf person's memories by matching synchronized physical movement with telepathy.** The deaf person's memory reproduces a particular sound and then telepathy projects it into the movement of an object that synchronizes this selected memorized sound with it, which then snaps this artificial sound into the conscious.

The sound coming from the deaf person's memory can be any sound they so chose to interject into the point of the physical movement of something with Flip synchronization. Obviously the correct matching natural sound would normally be better, as this sound is generally universally agreed upon as the one normally found in physical nature. A clock's ticking second hand gives off a sensation of movement somewhat similar to the illusion of sound technique.

Now with the telepathic sound imprint in mind, the deaf person focuses on something with movement such as a bird flapping its wings. When the bird's wings are at full down stroke the deaf person synchronizes this point with psychic energy and imagines reproducing a sound from his or her mind's memory that was implanted before with the help of another person or a group of peoples' summation telepathy and then interject this sound into the wings exact movements.

As said before a Spider's or Gecko's legs contacting a surface is even easier to do synchronizing the exact time the creature's feet touch the surface of something as it walks and adding the illusion of sound for this mind projection. This imagined sound of walking or stepping will be memorized by the deaf person through telepathy before hand and then retrieved from memory; then pushed out and synchronized into the creature's feet touching the surface of something by using telepathy projection. The creature's feet step rapidly but this is not a problem for the mind to synchronize this rapid motion with Flip and this is very easily done for each step observed interjecting artificial stepping sounds.

The sound projected out with telepathy and interjected into the creatures stepping here has an additional occurrence that makes this technique even better. **If there is more than 1 person involved summation telepathy will super amplify this**

imagined or real sound enhancing it and this artificial Flip sound is able to be heard by everyone for at least 100 meters radius inside their minds including the deaf people. This all sounds a little complicated but in actuality this is all very simple. This may take some time but this illusion of sound is a great thing that is completely available to all people deaf or people capable of normal hearing. **It may be noted here that real sound is also capable of being amplified with telepathy.**

I think deaf children that develop telepathy skills at an early age can learn to hear through this viewing of movement of an object or animal by adding synchronized sounds from their memories into this movement.

Deaf children may be able to dance to these artificial rhythmic telepathic sounds created from their memories and pushed and synchronized into something they are observing with movement or vibration.

This movement may also be accomplished by a strobe light or other types of movie projections that contain movement. Future video games may be created this same way for the deaf with lights flashing and vibrations supplying the synchronization and auxiliary helper for the illusion of telepathy sound; or equally said the illusion of hearing.

Percussion and Vibrations - Foot talking may be a way to teach deaf people primitive percussion sounds in their mind with the synchronization of the impact as the foot contacts the ground. Jogging or running will amplify even more the percussion vibrations going through the bones of the legs by the increase in shock energy moving up the spinal cord into the base of the brain. **This running will provide an excellent physical *auxiliary helper* for creating artificial sounds for the deaf jogger by the synchronization of these vibrations with telepathy implanted sounds from the deaf person's memory.** This synchronization of percussion vibrations also helps **retrieve** the sound thoughts from memory that have been previously inserted in memory of the deaf by telepathy using Psychic Energy.

Two deaf people or one deaf person in conjunction with a hearing person jumping together may provide the vibration synchronization energy to summate a thought from memories into the consciouses of both people participating resulting in hearing sound.

Children may dance to the internal mind's created telepathic sounds by running in place or jumping in place, the vibrations and percussion of the human body again being used for Flip synchronization by pushing memorized sounds into the synchronized percussion steps. Deaf people should easily be able to utilize jumping spinal column and bone shock vibrations to inject an artificial sound with the help of telepathy synchronization and amplification. Clapping your hands together solo or in co-operation with other people ("high fives") may be a way to utilize percussion synchronization for interjecting telepathy artificial sounds for the deaf. Deaf people moshing or mashing (dancing with high energy banging into each other) may have a good time communicating telepathic thoughts of sound by using the banging together vibrations.

Vibrations are much like Touching Flip and function as a physical auxiliary helper that will help **Synchronize the Illusion of Sound into the conscious of the deaf person and then record this artificial sound into their long term memory.** In the future the deaf person may use these same synchronized vibrations with psychic energy for retrieval of these previously implanted artificial thoughts from their memory back into the conscious for use as perceived artificial sound implanted from another person.

You must understand that foot talking, strobe lights, body motions, and sounds are just auxiliary helpers to help perform and synchronize telepathy; and if telepathy is mastered_none of these auxiliary helpers are needed to project any form of telepathy into another person's conscious mind. Artificial sound may be implanted into memory simply by Pure Telepathy and withdrawn by Pure or physical world auxiliary helpers. Some of us will always need physical world auxiliary helpers and we must simply learn to adjust and move on.

Sound Flip is a way that a normal hearing person may use to insert telepathy sounds in the deaf person's memory. The deaf person does not need to hear the sound that you the sender-teacher are using to synchronize your telepathy concept. **This auxiliary helper sound synchronizes and also gives your normal hearing mind confidence to insert a sound concept into the deaf person's conscious mind.** This sounds strange and complicated but it is not. Just do normal sound telepathy with the deaf person and the deaf person should hear your telepathy but not your physical sound auxiliary helper.

Solo Sound Flip - It is possible that a person may use headphones along with a portable CD or digital music player that is playing a strong music beat inside their headphones to sound Flip with. Only the person with the headset on hears the sound of the digital player enabling this person to perform sound Flip **solo** without any other person hearing their ***sound auxiliary helper.*** A person may also sound Flip words to the deaf person in this fashion of solo sound Flip.

Strobe Light - With practice a way may be found to synchronize telepathy into a strobe light by a teacher for insertion of thought or sound imprints into the consciouses of deaf people. Before the start of class everyday I think deaf children as well as mentally handicapped children should view passively a slow strobe light (it need not be viewed directly). This strobe light does not necessarily need to be bright; viewing this light casually for maybe just a few minutes to help synchronize the classes mind for easier telepathy and teaching before class comes to order.

Sign Language - A person may add a little **motion Flip to their hand sign language to accentuate it** and enhance it for communicating with deaf people. I think the percussion of slapping sign language into of the participating individual's hands would aid synchronization of the psychic energy for Flip transmission of concepts and also help accentuate the sign language.

Lip Synchronization of a word by the sender of telepathy but not speaking the word helps to project the word more clearly with mental telepathy with sound Flip or pure telepathy. So remember that this Lip Synchronization enhances other methods of telepathy and is not only used solely for the purpose of working with the deaf. **So we may take this method of Lip Synchronization for improving sound Flip and pure telepathy and apply this to helping deaf people communicate that functions exactly the same only now with telepathy the Lip Synchronization is used for communication in two ways.**

Note: Lip Sync for communicating with deaf people is nothing more than moving your mouth and lips with a bit of exaggeration trying to form words but without speaking any sound. This helps the internal conscious mind to think and hear the telepathy word projection a little clearer before pushing it out to others, and this Lip Sync is normally also used for the deaf.

The key to teaching deaf people the correct sounds inside their minds for forming word sounds may be through lip synchronizing and adding telepathy projection to the lip sync.

This addition of Flip to the normal lip synchronization technique for the deaf helps to add more power and clarity for improving this type of communication. This lip synchronization may be performed by another helping person other than the principle instructor using telepathy summation and listening to the sound of the word on a tape recording as the primary instructor lip syncs to the recording, or **another person may vocally pronounce the word in conjunction with telepathy to the deaf person.** A person may also play a percussion instrument along with the lip synching to help in the Flip transmission. Many combinations should be tried. **Words should be written on a white marker board and pointed to as the word is lip synced with telepathy.** The deaf person hears a telepathic sound but they do not know what word to associate the particular telepathic sound with; the pointing of the word while lip syncing matches these two things.

This telepathic summation through a master instructor with the addition of other people in the classroom such as volunteer parents may add extra psychic energy for the implanting of word sounds into the deaf student's memories. Some of the people in the group talking as they repeat the word and some listening as all people involved push out telepathy in unison with the synchronized sound of the word into the memories of the deaf students. This telepathy summation group will enter the conscious of the deaf students with a word sound using synchronization psychic energy as the ***vehicle*** to transport the telepathic thought into the deaf conscious. This will then record the telepathic sound into the long term memories of deaf children facilitating the learning of language skills by deaf students. We need to be open minded to the different combinations of telepathy techniques and try new things and report back to others with feedback. This stuff is all great but all so very new.

Everybody must be aware that all the above techniques for the deaf are not needed if a person possesses **Pure Flip**. Pure Flip goes directly into the conscious of the deaf person without auxiliary helpers that provide secondary synchronization.

Pure Flip may also write the message into the conscious of the deaf person through image projection. Alas, all people however will not be capable of doing Pure Flip or Image Flip in the near future and other simpler techniques must be used in conjunction with physical world helpers.

Help for Blind People

I have never yet worked with people that have been blind all their natural life. I have put images such as geometric shapes of triangles, squares, and also simple fruit shapes in about 50 blind peoples' mind that have had sight before they went blind. I am able to image project to the outside word Braille sphere images about the size of softballs for the blind to read. The blind always read my projected Braille spheres; at times I spin all the Braille balls in the outside environment for better detection. This is all true and we should all use our imagination with Flip and never give up trying to help people. If you are blind never doubt me because you have a purpose and possibly an obligation to take telepathy to new heights due to blind people having certain sense perceptions that are more acute than other people.

I have projected with telepathy various colors in quite a few blind peoples' mind in public centers of many cities and they seem to be able to touch the color I project that helps identify the color by touch. I am only guessing about this touching of color by blind people but this is very interesting. **Telepathy is capable of bypassing the conscious physical sensory input area from the outside world and go right to the mind's internal sense imaging.** I hope to work with more handicapped people in the future but again the Flip is new and I have not yet had time for all endeavors.

Sound Flip or Foot Talking are important tool for helping blind people that possess hearing capabilities to communicate with others. Blind people tapping their cane producing sound Flip or simply foot talking with a little sound added may be used while walking in the downtown area around people for casual communication and navigational instructions. Musical shoes, bells around children's ankles much like the Native American dancers use, metal taps on the bottom of shoes, or other sound producing devices may help the blind person to foot talk very easily to people around them as well as listen for foot talking navigational instructions from others in public.

A loose gravel area that makes loud crunching sounds in the blind childrens' schoolyard would be great for learning sound Flip and foot talking. I think in time the blind people of the world should be able to hear or sense the vibration of the foot talking when in close proximity to others in public with very little sound needed. Blind people develop a better sense of hearing, which gives them an advantage with sound Flip or foot talking synchronized sound perception. The blind people I have observed do so many fantastic things and they have helped me formulate a lot of ideas and have given me confidence in the wild imaginative progressive areas of the telepathy for helping others.

I have seen on television where a blind lady from Germany by the name of Sabriye Tenberken was teaching children in Tibet to play with a ball full of dried rice for sound location. This ball with rice is perfect for sound Flip, what a joy! This would be a great tool for blind people to learn spatial relations through sound telepathy location by playing soccer or other games with this ball filled with dried rice, which gives off a shaking sound for its location.

Many cities have traffic signal lights that aid the blind by emitting distinctive sounds for communicating the safe time to cross the street at the crosswalk. If a person (blind or sighted) touches the traffic light pole that emits this sound they can use it for sound Flip. By touching the light pole a person may direct sound Flip communicating among the people present at the intersection while at the same time blind people will be listening for this particular sound as it is meant to aid them. The sound coming from the traffic signals should be studied a little and set up to emit sounds that are conducive for sound Flip. I think a person touching the traffic light pole could give the blind person a better feel for the intersection by sound Flipping the depth perception and distance in number of meters to the curb stop. Attempting to regulate and direct the sound from the traffic light pole with ***Directional Flip***, which is the moving or aiming of sound Flip will help give increased depth perception and orientate the blind person while crossing the street. This scenario I am describing here of touching the traffic light pole and transmitting directional sound Flip is extremely easy to do, in fact it is the easiest telepathy stunt there is to perform, like **Magic for the Blind done by you the responsible caring person**.

Solo Sound Flip - A person may use headphones along with a portable digital or CD player that is playing a strong musical beat inside their headphones to sound Flip with. Only the person with the headset on hears the actual sound of the CD or digital player enabling this person to perform **sound Flip solo** without any other person hearing their **physical *sound auxiliary helper.*** A person may use this solo sound Flip to transmit directions to a blind person in the city in the distance by telepathy, say up to 100 meters orientating the blind person to their surrounding environment.

Motion Flip - The blind may attempt motion Flip and imagine a sound coming from the abrupt stoppage of hands, arms, or legs. **In time this motion Flip will lead to imaginary high fives with a normal sighted person that will help orientate the blind person to the corner along with pointing out obstacles and helping with depth perception.** The blind person may imagine slapping hands with another normal sighted person in the distance and when the imaginary slapping synchronization of the hand contact occurs then adding the illusion of sound from their imagination and memory as the hands slap together giving depth perception and orientation. These two people imagining slapping their hands may need to communicate beforehand with sound Flip for proper synchronization and orientation. This is a description of an image Flip that has touch and sound Flip both added to the image projection performed by a blind and sighted person. I am excellent at touching people at great distances with telepathy images with added sound and I think my blind friends who possess extra sensitivity and motivation will easily acquire to some degree this image Flipping or touch Flipping adding sound.

Aggressive Behavior or Hyperactivity

Children may be controlled a little and stress vented through mental telepathy. Communication is an outlet for over stimulus of the brain and telepathy communication will help to relieve some of the stress of aggressive or hyperactive children. A child may begin foot talking and then progress to sound Flip for a communication energy outlet that reduces over stimulus and stress in the child. Simply take the child for a walk and the both of you practice foot talking or possibly sound Flip that will ease the child's mind a little by communicating thoughts. Sound Flip with musical instruments would be nice for the child to vent energy and to learn with.

These aggressive or hyperactive children all have a hard time sitting still in one place to learn because of an over abundance of physical energy. However this energy can be utilized to learn the alphabet or learn to read by spelling simple words with foot talking or bouncing a rubber ball that emits sound Flip. Both foot talking and bouncing the rubber ball require children to physically move around that expends energy and also relieves stress that is ideal for the hyperactive child to learn along with being fun too.

Improved Muscle Co-ordination

I think the practicing of Motion Flip and Foot Talking will help improve the muscle co-ordination of handicapped people. These two techniques of telepathy are practiced normally in the course of everyday life. Daily movements of this type with the addition of these simple telepathy techniques will help muscles co-ordinate better by synchronization of movements with the mind. Walking, doing physical therapy, dancing to music or aerobic exercise, or any other sport while at the same time sound Flipping to music I think should aid in improving muscle co-ordination.

Running or jumping results in spinal column vibration and shock that helps in the synchronization of the telepathy in the conscious mind in relation to muscle movement.

Simple sports that require bouncing a ball and using sound Flip may also be beneficial for physical therapy improving muscle coordination with the mind. I think these telepathy exercises of motion may improve a crippled person's muscle coordination 10% to 15% or simply help in healing muscles properly.

Sports with Telepathy

<u>Mountain Climbing</u> - While I was hiking through some hills and steep mountains I found that when progressing up or down the **steep terrain** my solid placement of my foot was improved with projected sound telepathy and projected image touch telepathy. These techniques really improved the safety and efficiency of the climbing by maybe 25% especially when tired hiking up or down these steep hills or mountains.

This type of telepathy is initiated before the placement of the footstep, **imagining ahead of time the <u>feel of the future solid contact step</u> and also imagining what <u>sound the footstep</u> would make as it makes contact with the steep ground.** Quite similar to foot talking although communication is not the method we are after here rather solid and secure placement of the feet for climbing or descending mountains.

The steeper the mountain, the more telepathy will improve the efficiency of your step while climbing or descending when projecting an imagined future synchronized contact point on the hill along with the future imagined sound of the contact.

You need to slur both the future imagined solid foot contact and the future imagined sound together along with the feel of the real physical contact and the real sound emitted all flowing together as a continuous slurred time frame ending on the final real physical synchronized contact point. You will see what I mean when you practice this mountain climbing technique realizing that it is easy to attain this continuous slurred time frame similar to a musical slurred note; slurring the imagined and real concepts together on the final execution of the downbeat or physical contact.

Correct placement of the foot is also very important while walking on an uneven ocean reef beach composed of various types of extremely slippery rocks at low ocean tide. I have walked on many of these rocky beaches and some of the round and jagged rocks will twist your ankle and the flat rocks are at times very slippery with algae. Many times I practiced this same **look ahead foot projection** as I stepped out a secure course through the rocky reef with this above described telepathy. This practice can be tiring so I would suggest only doing ten minutes per hike on the reef. In time this concentrated effort here and there of telepathy look ahead projection for foot placement I put into each reef hike slowly became an automatic process eventually becoming a natural thing to do while walking on the ocean reef beaches.

Let me point out that this look ahead foot projection became an absolute necessity at times if you sprained or cut your ankle while diving on the ocean reef point and the tide is coming in splashing the rocks ahead making them extremely dangerous while walking back off the ocean reef point. If you should fall the rocks are extremely hard and sometimes jagged, which positively results in injury to some degree.

I had a native friend, Gallo of Guanacaste, Costa Rica, age 35, who was one of the best snorkel divers I have ever seen. Twice a week since childhood Gallo would walk the slippery reef at low tide and go spear fishing at the point with snorkel and fins. Gallo had tremendous skill at maneuvering among the rocks at low tide on the reef. One day Gallo and I were spear fishing on the reef when Gallo speared a giant red snapper and we got excited and headed back to town to show everyone. Gallo was moving along quickly as usual and I was almost as quick practicing my look ahead projection stepping because the reef was slippery when suddenly Gallo turned his ankle badly among the rocks. This awesome reef walker had succumbed to the rocks on this day and it was then I realized this look ahead projection on the reef rocks was no joke. I think that if the great Gallo reef walker had practiced look ahead projection walking on the reef that day he would had never slipped and fallen.

Runners - Synchronizing your running steps as they contact the ground, along with the shock and vibration of your body up the spinal column while at the same time inputting syllables of Flip words into these vibrations or steps will make for a nice form of meditation while running. This synchronized stepping will help to meditate and allow your mind to relax and maybe also free it from the pain of running. Jogging and Flipping words into your footsteps requires concentration but does give runners an optional "high" while jogging.

Types of Flip meditation while running I do think is going to be different for everyone but well worth the effort of practicing it on occasion. This shock contact of jogging and sound it emits may be amplified if the runner wears headphones or earplugs making these vibrations and sounds while running very easy to hear for the synchronizing of telepathy meditation.

As you practice telepathy over the years you may on a rare occasion hear your heartbeat echo thunderously as you are running, but do not be alarmed as everything in your body is running at a strenuous level but in perfect harmony with the universe and your heartbeat sounds extremely loud at times due to telepathy synchronization and amplification. I put this story in here because I love to jog now and then for exercise and on one occasion while I was running up a jungle hill in the tropics along the Pacific Ocean in Costa Rica my heart began to echo through the jungle, loud beyond belief due to my telepathy. I was pretty much alone when this occurred on a jungle hilltop along the Pacific Ocean. Although this was a random occurrence it was truly an amazing experience for me to hear my heart echo through the jungle and at first I freaked out for about 10 seconds but then I continued to run. After 10 seconds of startlement I realized that everything was running in perfect synchronization out here in nature and then the jogging turned into a thrilling moment. If you run long enough you may experience this same phenomenon with super amplified sounds; so try not to "freak out" as you are hearing **the power of your soul in perfect harmony with nature! Harmony of nature appears to be a type of synchronization here intertwining with psychic energy.**

Bouncing a basketball, hitting a hockey puck, ice skating, turning while snow skiing, race-car driving, hitting a tennis ball, kicking a soccer ball, hitting or catching a baseball are sports that all have sound to work telepathy with.

A football quarterback may synchronize the footsteps of his receiver with his mind making the reception of the pass a little easier. Tackling another football player while synchronizing both the touch Flip and sound Flip may also offer an opportunity to have fun as the shoulder pads and helmets collide with the sound and touch Flip.

Any sport that has footsteps or noise associated with it is a lot more fun and more adept with telepathy added.

As mentioned in the Psychology chapter playing a sport such as basketball and describing your problems to a friend as you bounce the basketball with sound Flip is very beneficial for relieving stress of simple problems and also preventing suicide.

Also mentioned in the previous chapter of Muscle Co-ordination was the method of bouncing a ball and using sound Flip that may be beneficial for physical therapy improving muscle coordination with the mind. I think these telepathy exercises of motion may improve a crippled person's muscle coordination 10% to 15% or simply help in healing muscles properly.

Progression with Flip on the Highway

Advanced Progression with Flip does not require a person to be in touch control of the noise or light generating device, yet they are still needed at this stage of Flip. I am not describing Pure Flip technique here, rather steps along way advancing to this higher stage of telepathy. The highway is a place that everybody occupies in normal everyday life quite frequently. Since people are constantly traveling on the highway regardless, this makes it a good place to practice Flip because of the noise occurring around vehicles and the flickering of vehicle headlights. People seem to enjoy these Flip communication games on the highway just for the fun of it and to kill the discomfort and boredom of travel.

Measuring or marking time with the aid of sound or light waves gives the human mind help with performing mental telepathy. Pulsating or flickering lights along with beats of sound on the highway give the mind physical help for synchronization and also add confidence to the human mind for easier thought transference between people. Although Flip is done easier with one beat of a sound or light pulse per syllable of word, two or more syllables of word can be attached to a single beat of sound or flicker of light as you master Flip.

Vehicles traveling down the highway create wind turbulence sound from underneath the vehicle along with tire and motor noise that is sometimes loud enough for an easy sound Flip; however this is not always true. Sometimes the sound generated from a moving vehicle on the highway is carried away by the wind or blocked by medians of cement or vegetation. To make it easier to hear these road noises a person's car window should be down a little bit enabling sound to enter the vehicle.

Let us first talk about cars traveling on the highway. Cars usually make enough continuous noise for attaching one syllable of word for sound Flip. A semi-truck has a longer duration of sound enabling you to push out two syllables of word into the noise of a single semi-truck. One syllable of word with the noise at the front of the truck and attach another syllable of word at the rear of the semi-truck's trailer as the final noise of the truck passes you by. More word syllables can be added than this but it is easier to start out with one syllable of word per car and two syllables for a semi-truck.

If you are walking through a neighborhood and a car passes you at a slow speed you may be able to Flip one syllable of word at the auto's noise as it is passing abreast you. With practice you may easily add another syllable of sound Flip as the auto completely passes by you with the end noise of the vehicle as this extra syllable of word Flip is made possible from the slow speed of the car in the neighborhood setting.

Also remember again **that a person who is in control of the noise making device may Flip with it and do it easier than somebody who is not in control of the noise producing device, normally the person in control of the vehicle (driver) will override your attempts at sound Flip with their own version.**

Two semi-trucks moving in opposite directions, passing each other abreast at a precise moment give off a flicker of light by the passing shadows of the large shading vehicles. So here you are capable of a solo syllable of light Flip here looking much like a strobe light effect and sound Flip may also be added, or a combination of both with the two semi-trucks passing in opposite directions.

There is a couple more ways for adding an extra syllable of Flip between two cars or trucks following one another headed in the opposite direction of your travel on the highway. Memorizing and then slurring the first car's sound in your mind, is one way to add another syllable of word sound Flip. The two cars cannot be following too far apart for this Flip trick, optimally one to five seconds apart. First you Flip the first car normally with noise (i.e. one syllable of word pushed into the first car's sound), then holding the first cars noise in your conscious mind and stretching this dwindling sound in your conscious memory much like slurring a particular musical note, you will then slur in a second syllable of Flip to about the center of the normally dead sound space between first car and the following second auto. As you are slurring the first car's sound in your mind you prepare yourself to push a syllable of thought right in to the middle of the two cars traveling in the opposite direction as you. **The reason for slurring the sound from the first car is to learn to Flip a word into the dead-space between the two cars that is emitting no sound as the second cars noise appears rapidly and this <u>fools the mind into thinking it had continuous noise to Flip with</u>.** The second car would then receive a 3rd syllable of word pushed into the normal sound generated by this second auto with sound telepathy.

Another Flip progression example is your vehicle traveling on the highway or expressway at say 60 miles per hour and adding sound Flip to the traffic again headed in the opposite direction on the highway. If a person uses car sounds with one syllable of word per car, he or she may **<u>bounce</u>** an extra syllable of word Flip in the dead space between two automobiles where no sound is occurring. You synchronize one syllable of word with sound Flip onto the first car's noise then you hold and slur this sound in your mind, you then imagine you are bouncing a ball on the ground in the space between the first and second auto. **About halfway between the two autos you bounce an imaginary ball off the pavement then attach a Flip word syllable to it.** When you hear the sound from the second car you then attach the normal sound Flip here with one syllable of word. This way you attain an extra syllable of Flip in the dead space between the two cars. You now get a total of 3 syllables of word for the two autos' separate sounds. The people that hear the Flip actually perceive the middle Flip as a slight bounce sound with a syllable of word attached to it much like a bouncing ball sound. The closer the cars are that are following each other, say 1 to 5 seconds, the easier the bounce Flip.

This bounce is a type of pure Flip, this being one of the ways pure Flip may be taught through this imaginary bouncing ball and attaching a pushed out word syllable at the exact point of the imaginary bounce on the highway. The bounce we are describing here also contains a faint image projection having no clarity or detail with a pure sound Flip attached when the ball hits the pavement. This very faint bounce image is easier to achieve than a clear formed image, which would take more skill and concentration. The projection is not clear nor does it possess detail but the desired effect of a faint object with a synchronized bounce contacting the highway while at the same time emitting a slight bounce sound is perceived. These two car tricks are forms of pure telepathy because no auxiliary helpers are used, instead they are totally generated in the internal mind's imagination and the mind is tricked into confidence for performing Flip here by using the former sound from memory.

The Flip when used during a dangerous situation on the highway will highlight the problem vehicle to another person sometimes avoiding an accident. When you are afraid you will automatically project mental telepathy just a little better because of the added emotion that pulls together more psychic energy. So remember even if you don't care for Flip, when your family is in a dangerous situation yelling a command in your mind for a course of action will prevent an accident out to 1000 meters or more. By concentrating on projecting an alert to where the attention is needed your high emotional telepathy has a good chance of working because of the added psychic energy the high emotions produce during a threatening situation and this enables a person to push a telepathy warning out a lot easier.

In traffic a person should Flip-project looking ahead on the highway, imagining and visualizing making a moving operation in traffic such as passing. **Although a person may not be able to do mental telepathy projection very well you should still try to visualize your future traffic pass by lightly thinking about the pass**

ahead of time and pushing it out from your conscious focus onto the highway ahead before you pull out into the passing lane. This will enable other vehicles in traffic to pick up on your ***mental telepathy drift*** that is weakly being transmitted all around you. Although this ***mental drift*** is not totally clear or powerful all the people around you in traffic will feel it to some degree making the highway safer for you and your family. Note: Mental Telepathy Drift is incomplete Telepathy or weak telepathy because the ***synchronization*** for whatever reason is not completely learned for transmission.

I would just like to add that the telepathy nickname **"Flip"** comes from just tossing mental telepathy out into traffic noise or "**Flipping" it out in traffic. Just "toss" it out.** Thus the name of this book comes from the early beginnings of telepathy as I was walking on highway pedestrian overpasses hearing and synchronizing the sounds around the highways and city streets. I also like the name Flip for its possible use as the acronym F.L.I.P that stands for (Future Link Intelligent People).

Awareness

As we practice Flip, which is a true form of extrasensory perception our senses begin to be a little more acute in picking up stimulus from the senses both in the internal mind along with all the physical input from the external world. **Noise pollution becomes more apparent from such sources as airplanes and city buses as you practice telepathy more and more.** Human footsteps become a little more noticeable, squirrels running, geckos running, anything concentrated on will be amplified now with mental telepathy. Smog pollution of the city will also be amplified quite a bit more making smog a more noticeable problem.

It is amazing and lots of fun learning to Flip a darting dragonfly's motion and sound or even a humming bird's rapidly beating wings sound and darting motion, which amplifies the sounds and motions of the creature. Another example would be simply the increased awareness of the wind's sound and feel due to practicing Flip. Colors of the rainbow as mentioned in the Summation Chapter are also more pronounced with the help of others.

In addition, emotions are amplified with telepathy especially when projecting something that has high sentimental value or violence attached to it. You will find at times that you are over-emotional doing this type of telepathy; as the telepathy will heighten your sensations of emotion and violence.

As mentioned before in the Highway Progression Section; mental telepathy "push out" from the conscious mind is accomplished a lot easier in a high emotional situation. The example used before was trying to avoid a traffic accident thereby preventing injury to you or your family. To reiterate; even though a person may not be able to do mental telepathy projection, concentrating on your visualized pass and lightly thinking about pushing it out of your mind will enable others to pick up on your mental drift around you. Although this mental telepathy drift is not totally clear all the people around you in traffic will feel it to some degree making the highway safer for you and your family. **This mental telepathy drift is made available by an increase in the awareness in the world of other people's thoughts as more people use telepathy; enabling facilitation for perception and transmission of psychic energy through the combined power of the Universal Mind.**

As a person begins to get better at mental telepathy they start to feel the nakedness of his or her conscious thoughts through clear synchronized telepathy or unsynchronized mental telepathy drift. You begin to notice how your mind becomes more transparent and all your conscious thoughts are able to be viewed by the public world. You are a little afraid at first of what people might think of your dirty thoughts. Then after a few months you no longer consider what other people think of your everyday thoughts. You realize you are just a human whose thoughts shock no one who is able to view them with ***telepathy transparency*** as long as evil or violent thoughts are not ***dwelled*** on no one seems to care. In time I think you will feel the pressure of a higher intelligence checking on you; the universal mind that contains a ***world conscience*** that helps you to choose moral and more beneficial thoughts for you as well as society. If you are ashamed to share your conscious thoughts publicly, then you are generally thinking incorrect thoughts.

Mental telepathy will make the world aware of all the violence we as society has downloaded from the media and cinema into our memories. We will examine each other's minds through telepathy and find that they are just full of violence, maybe too much at times.

The whole world practicing mental telepathy will lead to more sensitive emotions and better treatment of others through the transparency of the conscious mind by telepathy that enables the running of the world conscience for moral comparison and in addition policing incorrect thoughts.

Practicing telepathy also increases efficiency and productivity in the mind for problem solving; this made possible by synchronizing one's thoughts that seems to improve the mind much like an engine running out of tune that is put back in time. **Flip also opens other dimensions in the internal mind for added resources for problem solving and concept construction by linking an infinite number of memories together by psychic energy.**

I would like to recount an impressive experience in the mountains out in Arizona, United States. I was in a large sawmill on a windy day standing on top of a high truckload of fresh cut lumber observing the wind blowing sawdust along the pavement of the sawmill between the buildings. The swirling sawdust blowing across the pavement took on the shape of miniature spiral galaxies one right after another about 30 seconds apart each about ten feet in diameter. One of my favorite Flips is "Peace on Earth" so at this time I began to interject the words peace on earth with Flip into the **swirling wind touching my face,** the **sound of the wind blowing over my ears,** and into the **motion of the spiral sawdust.** This natural experience of awareness contains a combination of Flips being the feel of the wind, sound of the wind, and the sight motion of the swirling sawdust.

I wrote a little poem about this experience that gives insight into the magic of thought transference and the harmony with nature as you push telepathy out into every sensation of nature. Flipping in nature definitely results in a mellow high at times with nature's power put into harmony with your mind's thoughts.

The soothing vibrations of the wind against my skin.
Resonating sounds as the wind swept across my face, rushing over my ears.
Ten-foot diameter pinwheels of fresh cut sawdust appear one after another,
Swirling on the pavement continuing with the course of the wind.
Evoking visions of spiral galaxies spinning in the heavens,
By some unseen spatial wind driving them deep into the universe.

Judgement of Telepathy around Family and Close Contacts

Parents will have to learn not to think a lot of violent thoughts because this is modeling the wrong behavior that will be easily learned by telepathy to their children. These violent or other socially incorrect thoughts modeled by parents will meet with social disapproval for the parents and their children. The new generation of children will be picking up on their parents' socially incorrect thoughts more readily through these new telepathy practices as well as simple ***mental telepathy drift***. A parent who is readying for the birth of a child in this **New World of Telepathy** must change their ways of thinking because their child's world has changed for the better with a little more social judgment of their incorrect conscious thoughts.

Parents modeling silly thoughts will also meet with the recording of these thoughts as being inappropriate. In the future things that instill silly thoughts in the minds of children that in the past proved to be great clean humor are all now going to be judged to be in excess as well as wrong.

Let us make clear why at one time in the past this silly behavior from the parents along with a little violence through the media was completely normal and probably a good time shared by the family ridding one's house of boredom. This change is incorporated through the thoughts of family members and close friends being more open for public inspection as **telepathy amplifies and makes a person's conscious mind's thoughts more transparent.**

These violent or silly thoughts that for the most part remained hidden before the invention of telepathy will now be leaked out more often on a daily basis in the family and around other close personal contacts and therefore these thoughts will be **judged more frequently** with this telepathy inspection. **Parents' teaching their children bad habits by modeling silly and violent thoughts will be guilty of teaching mental child abuse to their children as telepathy begins to take hold in the world now.**

Mental telepathy creates a new beginning in the world with all peoples' conscious thoughts becoming increasing more transparent over time; transparent especially to your closest friends and contacts. The world population is learning more and more telepathy facilitating the reading of thoughts from all people in the world as more time goes on eventually becoming an automatic transparency of conscious thought. As the telepathy in the world becomes stronger the necessity for totally clear thought transference will not always be needed to pick up on another person's general conscious concepts and these concepts may simply be **picked up through weak unsynchronized telepathy or mental telepathy drift.**

In addition another person's telepathy viewing of your pre-conscious thoughts may supply **summation energy, which increases psychic energy.** This summation energy adds more clarity and power to these pre-conscious concepts enabling these thoughts to now be recognized snapping them into the conscious of both participants (the originator of the thought and the person telepathically observing your pre-conscious thoughts and summating them with additional psychic energy). In addition the summation telepathy of two or more minds adds missing pieces to these pre-conscious concepts also increasing conscious recognition energy resulting in breaking the energy threshold and into the conscious now.

These two things, transparency of conscious thought and summation energy amplify thoughts that normally would be hidden from view and judgment without the addition of telepathy. This viewing of conscious thoughts is even easier to achieve by the knowledge and familiarity of close acquaintances and family. The majority of the time the thoughts that are made transparent for telepathic examination are the concepts currently in the conscious gallery and the most recently discarded thoughts from the conscious now residing in the pre-conscious zone that still have a little residual recognition power. These discarded thoughts into the pre-conscious also have residual power for 2 or 3 minutes, more recognition time added to the concept if the thought was striking.

When a thought is viewed in someone else's mind other than your own, severe judgment is passed for some reason upon this concept. This thought in another person's conscious normally would never have been viewed before the invention of telepathy and therefore never scrutinized and judged.

The originator's thought builds slowly in his or her conscious thereby desensitizing the thought as it is created rather than the instant shock effect of total recognition by another objective mind. Maybe because this thought has now entered another person's mind other than the originator of this particular concept and here in the stranger's mind it is now too threatening for the stranger's own conscience and now the non-originator of the concept is required to judge and many times now condemn the originator's thought or thoughts if they seem incorrect.

On the other hand it is possible that the **objective view of another person's thoughts is always more critical by not knowing how these thoughts are going to be applied** or if the thought is to be discarded as fantasy. **A subjective view is the perception the originator takes of his or her conscious thoughts and is not so critical possibly judged only as a passing thought because of the desensitizing process occurring during building of this particular concept, and the conscious may have intentions of ignoring and discarding.**

As mentioned before in the Emotions chapter a person should always try to think nice thoughts especially when around family and friends because through the everyday exercise of telepathy some thoughts will begin to leak out of your mind without the effort of conscious push out. Flip could easily leak out into your foot talking or as you are washing the dishes through sound Flip using the running water's sound. This leaking out of thought transference while washing dishes sounds silly but it will happen quite frequently. **There will naturally be a few times that bad**

things will come out of your mind with telepathy and a person should try to restrain these bad thoughts around family and friends. Many bad things with be projected accidentally with Flip telepathy but not meant to intentionally hurt a person and should be ignored unless the frequency becomes great, **we are not perfect human being as of yet**. A close acquaintance or family member should also be a little forgiving when observing conscious thoughts with telepathy as the human animal thinks many bad thoughts and even at times bad thoughts of people you love; this is normal and should be overlooked unless it is continued to be observed.

This viewing of conscious mental thoughts necessitates more control of incorrect thoughts in one's mind in the future especially around your close contacts as they will be able to home in on your mind frequently and judge your thoughts a lot more with the advent of telepathy.

With all this **amplification of silly thoughts** also comes a strange occurrence of not being able to pick on oneself so much anymore for laughs because this is also amplified. If you pick on yourself in a jesting way with telepathy another person can amplify this silliness even more with summation telepathy making you hurt yourself more than you intended especially if it is an image projection. Other self-defeating thoughts can also be turned against you with mental telepathy and you must learn to control these hurting and other non-productive thoughts or they will be used all against you.

Family and close acquaintances will now be able to pick up on your love more easily too.

Pure Flip

As one gets to be proficient in mental telepathy over the course of a lifetime it is possible for a person to move to one of its highest levels, which I call "PURE" Flip. Flip will probably begin to be an integral part of everyday life and in fact may just catch on like wildfire in a short time especially with the writing of this book. Therefore a constant dabbling in Flip over the years will begin to make many people extremely adept at various aspects of mental telepathy; especially if telepathy was started early in one's life.

I named this highest level of Flip "PURE" because there are no auxiliary helpers to aid in the synchronization of psychic energy for telepathy transmission. No sound, motion, light, or other physical energies to help the telepathy projection of conscious thought only pure psychic energy of the internal mind for secondary synchronization. **Also, it must be noted that the breaking of words into syllables is no longer needed with Pure telepathy transmission.** Pure telepathy has learned to enter the universal mind without auxiliary helpers, which is the goal of telepathy to use only the human mind.

Some of these physical world auxiliary helpers are at times not really helping your telepathy with added energy for synchronization rather they simply provide confidence to trick the mind into thinking it can perform mental telepathy. Many times an illusion seems real to the internal mind in every way; able to imitate the same effect as the real life senses.

Pure Flip is a higher form of mental telepathy that derives its source for synchronization energy solely from the inner mind's psychic energy. Pure thought transference is totally internalized and constructed in the conscious mind then pushed out into the physical world or projected into another person's conscious mind via the universal mind. Pure thought concepts may also originate as a weak pre-conscious thought powered up by the focus of another person on your pre-conscious thoughts that between the two of you now has enough psychic energy for this concept to now be recognized in the consciouses of both people sometimes entering the conscious of the originator for the second time.

I do not want to frustrate any one that has a hard time with any mental telepathy. Not everybody in the world is going to be able to do pure Flip but as long as you can comprehend what it is and maybe do a little foot talking and sound Flip, what the heck you're there participating in telepathy communication. **On occasion some unskilled people will have random thought transference in the pure form and perhaps over great distances.**

Although all people may not achieve transmission of pure Flip the entire population is capable of its reception. Pure Flip is fainter and quieter in the brain then sound telepathy but it is totally perceivable as the concept you intended to transmit. If the Flip is lacking in power, volume, clarity, or even incomplete in content then the receiver's memories might match pieces to the incomplete concept or amplify it. The receiver's memories would then enhance the concept intended by the originator as both parties contribute bits and pieces for better clarity and added volume. This I give the name **summation telepathy of psychic energy** because it is the sum of two or more minds and not a single individual.

When a person practices pure Flip or any other type of thought transference, medium concentration is needed. Heavy concentration seems to be defeating most of the time for Flipping, medium concentration optimal.

Pure Mental telepathy is generally the same as spoken internal conscious thought and the clearer the thought is spoken inside the originator's mind then the clearer it is able to be projected out and perceived. This internal spoken thought is the same as silent reading that with practice is learned to be pushed out of the mind as mental telepathy and over time with decreasing effort.

Counting or reading inside your mind silently is considered to be a higher form of intelligence than reading aloud and we all learn this as young children. Silent prayer has sometimes been referred to as mental telepathy with God. Some religions will also refer to the universal mind as God; this being a personal preference and this book does not denote what philosophy a person should accept.

As time progresses a master Flipper seems to need less and less concentration to project telepathy out to the environment and into the consciouses of other surrounding people by pure techniques. This lack of concentration eventually leads to the master Flipper's conscious thoughts being totally transparent to the public and no longer is the push out of thought needed from the master's conscious mind for its telepathic reception.

All people in close proximity (100 meter radius) in relation to a master transmitter of Flip can recognize the master's normal conscious thought flowing through their mind with telepathy as a totally clear concept, faint but clear. **People will hear and see the master Flipper's conscious thoughts in the immediate surrounding area but will not know the identity of this individual leaking these thoughts with telepathy transparency.** By deduction it would be easy to figure out who this is in a small group or family setting. It is possible to hide your conscious thoughts once you attain this stage of master telepathist but this takes extreme concentration and becomes tiresome very quickly allowing you to hide your thoughts for maybe only 2 or 3 minutes. So the majority of time master telepathist's conscious thoughts lay open for inspection by the public and in a short time the identity of the originator of these thoughts is established.

Super violent thoughts or high emotional thoughts as said before possess a lot of psychic recognition power and will be impossible to hide; as said before maybe only for a few minutes it is that tough to maintain control over these violent or highly charged emotional thoughts. The identity of all master telepathists with violent thoughts entering into your conscious focus will be easily made almost immediately due to the violent thoughts possessing extreme high psychic energy.

The transparency of the human conscious mind seems to me to be the intended goal for all intelligence in the universe mankind using this transparency for observing all conscious thoughts and helping to choose the correct thoughts by the moral pressure of the world conscience along with the logic contained inside the universal mind.

Pure telepathy is transmitted, received, and repeated back vocally by the receiver to the originator all simultaneously. Sometimes the pure Flip technique concept is sent back vocally by the receiver totally before it is completely transmitted from the originator's mind. There is some kind of time gain here that I am at a loss to comment on partly because mental telepathy is new and a little more work is in order. Thought transference goes against the laws of physics because the recognition time and response time are unaccounted for in the time measurement of mind transference concepts as psychic energy thoughts occur simultaneously in all surrounding consciouses, and sometimes faster than simultaneous, which translates into slight time gain here.

A few people are so quick at repeating thoughts vocally back to me; I barely know I thought them or sent them with telepathy; Astounding! This very quick vocal repetition of telepathic thought is very irritating for my mind; however if all people practice pure Flip than this super fast telepathy communication would not be irritating as there is no vocals involved here.

Aiming of pure Flip and controlling sound location*;* it is possible to aim pure Flip to go to any location within a 1000 meter radius clearly without any auxiliary noise, light, or motion needed only the human mind. If someone vocalizes or makes another sound you may utilize this sound and move their voice or sound around to seem to come from another location other than the original sources location.

Remember pure Flip does not need sound to transmit but if sound is present it may be re-directed and utilized by a person capable of pure Flip.

Pure Flip is capable of creating its own sound from memory inside the mind. Again, it can be anywhere within a 1000 meter radius that the telepathic artificial imagined voice retrieved from your memory or any other sound may be transmitted solely by psychic energy synchronized with your memory's sound. The further the telepathy sound projection in the outside world the harder it is to sound clear. Note: The distances given in this book are generalizations, and I personally think I could Flip the space shuttle in orbit above the earth as a visual reflective satellite giving you an idea about its limits. The thing that makes Flipping sounds or images into the space shuttle so simple is the fact that I can actually see the space shuttle at night as a satellite reflecting sun at night, same as the moon does. This gives my mind 100% confidence that I can put telepathy images into the shuttle in space orbit at night as I can visually see and aim the telepathy at a known physical location.

Any imitated person's voice is easier to project and move around than just a plain sound. A person's own voice is not as well memorized as someone else's voice. For this reason it is easier to sound project someone else's voice from your memory rather than use your own voice from memory. Using distinctive voices of movie stars in your voice direction Flip helps tremendously because they are all well memorized and distinctly known by both you and the receiver. Another person's voice may even be moved to appear as if coming out of your own mouth or redirected to another person's mouth within the Flip radius. If so desired you may voice over their voice with your Flip thought words changing the perceived sounds. Of course these complicated Flip techniques require a more learned telepathist or master at telepathy.

Clapping your hands and then attaching a Flip word syllable to the past conscious memory of an echo of the clap from the previous second or two is another example of pure Flip from memory. The **conscious memory will remember all recent**

physical world sensory information for up to five seconds in the conscious that may be used in the application of telepathy.

Pure Flip is also a way for the human mind to fight back keeping the mind healthy. In some circumstances an individual is not capable of offering a verbal rebuttal due to social circumstances or the need to show respect for a dominant boss. Here mental telepathy is in order. Although just a thought would offer some solace; a concentrated push out of the rebuttal with pure telepathy although nonverbal offers much satisfaction to the human psyche. Although this telepathy rebuttal does not provide the same amount of **stress release** as normal vocals it is close and you will not get in trouble with a Flip rebuttal like vocals would. We all need to show respect but when mutual respect is lacking the mind will reach for telepathy as a rebuttal and may be justified.

Pure Telepathy can project all six senses listed in the following power order;

1- Sound, 2- Sight, 3- Touch, 4- Emotion, 5- Taste, 6- Smell.

Let me point out that the power order of measurements here are close and not super far apart in range. Notice that emotion with telepathy rates ahead of taste and smell in the power reception for the senses giving support that emotion is the 6th **sense**. Emotions has its own chapter in this book.

Speed of light telepathy versus speed of sound telepathy. This is a unique experience that uses auxiliary helpers but I think it belongs here.

A crew of 4 men were working on a railroad track driving spikes against the steel rails with a large sledge hammer about 250 meters down the railroad track from my observation point. I noticed the impact of the sledgehammer as it came into contact with the railroad spike and I Flipped this light image synchronization point. After a moment following the sight of the hammer strike came the sound of the strike and I then Flipped a syllable of word with the sound of the hammer.

So I was able to differentiate between light and sound because the sound traveled slower than light and I synchronized both with Flip projection. Here illustrates the problem with physical world auxiliary helpers such as foot talking or sound Flip; they both require the conscious to wait on the thought while pure Flip does not wait for physical limitations. The internal mind's pure capabilities transmit a psychic thought directly into the universal mind instantly bypassing the physical world and its time restrictions.

Pure Flip should be able to go around the world with a trained significant other or close friend. The receiver has to be trained for this long distance mental telepathy but many people do it well. I think that with practice I could go around the world with a trained person without the help of the phone or television, which are types of auxiliary helpers. Pure Flip is capable of going through solid objects and I also have Flipped 10 meters underwater to a distance of 1000 meters away clearly hundreds of times. I can synchronize a television program with pure telepathy or images that would to go around the world instantly with Flip telepathy.

The physical reference points made by the Chandler Radio Telescope along with the visible stars of the universe are also simple auxiliary helpers giving confidence to the mind that energy has been there and back making them physical measured distances or reference points. There is no distance too great when two minds are interconnected for telepathy; the two minds communicate instantly at infinite distance with psychic energy. Telepathy is able to transverse the entire distance of the universe, which is 10 billion light years according to the Chandler telescope and back in less than .1 (one tenth) of a second. This total distance there and back from the farthest corner of the universe is of course 20 billion light years. This measured distance and the speed of light give us an approximation of the speed of psychic energy, 20 billion light years in less than one tenth of a second. Of course these figures are of little importance because the internal mind's thought processes when using psychic energy do not pay attention to physical law. If however there is another skilled known telepathist in the farthest corner of the universe at this present time then telepathy with this person would instantly be very easy to do at present as the other person would serve as a reference point for confidence. To some people a skilled person in the farthest corner of the universe could be thought of as the creator and telepathy communication with the creator is known as meditation or prayer.

Telepathy does not need physical form in the universe nor is it required to obey the principles of physical law; it only has to be logical. Pure thought or pure telepathy bypasses the physical world going mind to mind and this makes the physical world not a factor for limitations. The internal human mind refuses to obey the outside world's physical limitations when using psychic energy.

Telepathy has increased our area of thought to encompass our entire universe and quite possible all areas of the time dimension forward and backwards without physical appliances. **Before the invention of Pure thought transference all the thoughts in the world had to have some type of physical presence to be transported beyond the normal voice range.** Such devices as the telephone, computer, books, and the physical movement of the human brain from place to place but these however are all physical appliances or physical transportation of the thought concept and are not needed with Pure Flip Psychic Energy in the universes of the internal mind.

The two necessary requirements for transmission of telepathy to the farthest corner of the universe are the known conscious address of the receiver or familiarity with its memories, and confidence provided by a physical reference point that would be satellite physical measuring devices of radiation and light.

Psychic Logic Block Theory

Logic Block Theory is a telepathy concept based on the internal mind's imaginative capabilities limited only by the rules of logic. **A newly constructed telepathy logic block of the internal mind must agree with all other true proven telepathy logic foundation blocks that have come before it.** These logic blocks are all related and dependent on one another, this making the telepathy a form of relative thinking (built on other thoughts). Using these logic blocks we are able to build complex internal mind functions from assembling many of these basic logic blocks together for accomplishing mental tasks. If a faulty telepathic logic block is inserted in the building sequence then function failure will result and the system will fall back to the primary well known logic blocks. This falling back will cause confusion, low confidence and lost time resulting in the failure of newly created reality concepts holding true on the planet earth due to faulty telepathy reasoning.

Psychic Logic Blocks for the internal mind do not have to obey physical law only logical reasoning.

Creation of a Psychic Logic Block

1 - Conscious formation of Telepathic Concept through imagination.

2 - Name and categorize.

3 - Logic evaluation.

4 - Commit to memory by rough written draft.

5 - Comparison to other former psychic logic blocks for agreement.

6 - Psychic Energy trials with other people for validation that the telepathy concept is real and functioning.

7 - A Gel period for the new reality to harden and concretize in everybody's mind, (a few months to a few years).

8 - Formal statement and writing.

By building solid telepathic logic blocks one on top of the other mankind will be able to harness the human internal minds potential. Whatever happens inside the human body can be regulated with telepathy by synchronizing everything with psychic energy in the mind. We will someday cure cancer, A.I.D.S., and all other diseases that are formed inside our body with mental telepathy through the building process of these logic blocks. This curing of the body of its diseases will be accomplished with the help of synchronized Psychic Energy in the conscious mind that carries thoughts and commands throughout the body, psychic energy being the basis of telepathy energy and theory. Whatever the internal body creates logic dictates that the internal human mind aided by psychic telepathy will be able to regulate it or correct the situation.

When filled with doubt a person must re-examine the previous logic blocks I have created and written in this book as proven foundation blocks. I have laid a strong foundation with many proven logic blocks to build forward and progress inside the internal mind. When in total doubt a person can fall back to my proven logic blocks but no further. I have created new realities and they have been accepted and proven as real by millions of people of this world. We have created logical new realities in the 21st century and we will continue to create new realities for helping mankind with imagination and the True Flip Logic Blocks laid down in this book.

We will cure diseases of the human body in the future by building step by step with these logic blocks. I am totally positive that the mind will cure the body of all diseases but we cannot jump ahead and fall back on ourselves with missing or faulty logic blocks in construction of future complex mental telepathy tasks.

In the past we were all looking for clues in the mental telepathy field and hoping. Now with the foundation skills put forth in this book "FLIP" we build on these foundations with solid logic blocks; one by one and vague clues are no more needed in the telepathy field. Mankind is only limited by the internal minds capability to form logic blocks, and the confidence and imagination for these intangible concepts.

Hiding Socially Incorrect Thoughts or High Emotional Thoughts

Violent thoughts in the conscious mind are difficult to hide because they possess a large amount of psychic energy, even at times to be intense with this violent psychic energy. Love is also high in psychic energy and will impossible to hide by normal people for periods of more than 2 or 3 days before being picked up with ***mental telepathy drift*** by the people around you. If I the author had violent or love thoughts they would be picked up in 2 or 3 minutes by others because my mind has been trained over the years for transparency and it is impossible for me to hide my thoughts more than 2 or 3 minutes because masters of telepathy have transparency.

A large amount of people will begin practicing telepathy and this will start to synchronize their conscious mind's thoughts through foot talking and sound Flip techniques over a few months time. This large number of people in society practicing Flip will enable people with just a little telepathic ability to begin to pick up on various thoughts from others with telepathy. The more people that learn the techniques of mental telepathy in the world, the easier Flip will be for all people to perceive and perform this telepathy. The more people practicing telepathy the more powerful the **universal mind** becomes increasing the potential for synchronized psychic energy availability for telepathy scanning of other people's thoughts.

This former statement is called the **Social Learning Theory of Telepathy**, which makes it easy for Flip in the very near future by requiring less and less effort as more people learn and practice telepathy. **All of the telepathy seems to be working from a single mind in the universe with billions of physical brains plugged into it and pumping synchronized psychic energy with thoughts attached in and out of the universal mind. So the more people using the universal mind the easier the telepathy becomes.**

Family members along with significant others will be able to easily detect your violent or other socially incorrect thoughts right away or most certainly over a few days as your thought transference is easily picked up on by individuals close to you. These family members may be able to amplify these incorrect thoughts even more by forming one mind in the home as all the shielding of minds will be lowered in the family environment. **As the conscious shielding of family members in the home is lowered by trust their minds will flow together facilitating telepathy summation.** This will make perception of all conscious thoughts in the home easier with this telepathy summation and also allow for the push out of love in the home environment as an automatic daily occurrence.

People who are your close acquaintances or co-workers will also begin to pick up on your violent or socially incorrect thoughts readily. A person as yourself may try hard to deceive non-**familiar personas and may succeed in hiding some violent thoughts as long as there are no high emotions attached that would give added psychic energy to break threshold into the conscious awareness of the *non-originator* with this violent thought.** Over time your violent thoughts will most certainly arise again and again until they are finally exposed into the conscious awareness of others through telepathy.

Super violent thoughts or high emotional thoughts such as love possess a lot of recognition power and will be almost impossible to hide, possibly only for a few minutes it's that tough to maintain conscious control over these super violent or highly charged emotional thoughts that possess a lot of Psychic Energy.

Socially wrong thoughts also possess almost as much mental telepathy power as violent thoughts through the emotion of guilt along with the constant worry about getting caught by the police. Worrying about a situation means that the troubling thought constantly re-enters the conscious that makes it more readily perceived by others over time. Socially wrong thoughts may also be viewed as a type of violence against society.

People that became good at mental telepathy will have to concentrate greatly to hide any thought in their conscious mind. Hiding thoughts by people possessing some telepathy skill will be extremely hard to do for two reasons; the first drawback of hiding thoughts is the requirement of the person to turn his or her volume of thoughts down to practically nil that makes his or her internal thoughts less clear in their conscious mind. This low internal conscious thought volume handicaps a person's thinking process resulting in fuzzy concepts. The second drawback to hiding conscious thought is that this hiding can be maintained only for a few minutes requiring great amounts of concentration to accomplish this hiding task diminishing other thought construction.

The **World Conscience** that consists of the total accumulation of physical brains in the world that forms a single telepathic moral mind allows all people to know your conscious thoughts. This collective conscience as it develops more over time will eventually put more and more pressure on a person's mind to follow the furrow of normalcy in society.

Deviant people will migrate among people who think the same as themselves trying hard to reduce this increased social pressure, following the old saying birds of a feather flock together. These groups should pick up a violent label quite rapidly with telepathy increasing in the future as they amplify their thinking even more as a group.

It would seem anyone in the future that is immune to the weight of the world conscience would have to be considered anti-social and quite possible viewed as a sick sociopath able to carry out any type of crime against the good of man and should thereby be easily monitored constantly by their violent thoughts.

World Conscience (Moral Memory)

As a person becomes more proficient with telepathy he or she becomes increasing more capable of quiet thought transference yet at the same time more receptive to others; this is called **Pure Flip**. This quiet improved thought transference requires a lot less effort and concentration to transmit. **Although the perceived sound volume of a person's conscious thoughts who is proficient at pure Flip are quiet now, the telepathy still maintains good quality of sound and clear images in the mind-to-mind transference and its perception.** The master of telepathy can easily transmit loud perceived volume if he or she wishes but this is not necessary for clear reception as a person gains their skills in Pure Telepathy. This Pure or new quiet version of telepathy is so it does not interfere with another person's thinking when ethics rules are followed by the people involved.

Also, as the telepathist gains skill, his or her conscious thoughts become more and more transparent without putting forth the effort of telepathy transmission allowing all people for approximately 100 meters around the master to view their conscious thoughts.

Even if other people viewing the skilled telepathist's mind are not capable of the transmission of mental telepathy they are able to view the master's transparent conscious concepts. It will for the moment remain difficult to point out the identity of the individual who is leaking these conscious thoughts to us. As said before by deduction in small groups and family settings along with the known proximity to the individual will enable others to link his or her transparent thoughts together with his or her identity. And of course super violent thoughts will definitely identify the originator as well as highly emotional charged thoughts, which are both too powerful to hide for any more than a few minutes even by a master or an amateur telepathist. In addition the more you try to hide a thought the more psychic energy it accumulates due to the energizing by guilt emotions.

As said before; all the people in the world exert moral pressure through the total accumulation of physical brains forming a world conscience inside the universal mind through the practice of telepathy. This pressure would be a common sense obligation to think about choosing the right choice by morals and logic; which is the contents of the world conscience chosen by the majority thinking of what the world considers correct. These morals contained in the universal mind leads to the forming of the ***world conscience or collective conscience.*** This conscience includes the ethical and emotional sensitivity regarding treatment of other people in the world. Conscience by definition is another type of long term memory storing correct logic and social morals, 99.99% of the time logical thoughts are going to be moral or ethical also. This world conscience memory could be referred to as a **living collective conscience storing morals and logic** for all humans to compare their thoughts to; an archetype moral mind in the form of a living long term memory located inside the telepathic universal mind.

The world conscience moral memory is brought forward into the conscious mind's awareness of all people in the world who will monitor one another's thoughts through telepathy transparency and cross-matching them to these archetypes of morals. As we begin to use telepathy in the 21st century this monitoring by the world conscience will most likely for now be accomplished by people in close physical proximity to you. At times people from the other side of the world will monitor your thoughts but most likely in the beginning phases of telepathy it will be someone probably within 100 meters of you.

In the near future if ethics rules are not followed when telepathy scanning another person's mind; then a person initiating this breech of ethics would begin to feel the weight of the social conscience initiating punishment of some type. This is where the quiet yet more powerful telepathy comes in, the fact that all people will feel or recognize telepathic policing of their conscious thought, though no interference in one another's thought processes takes place when correct social morals are followed. This will occur as the brain monitors all quiet telepathy around it subliminally unless the thoughts are not correct and then the **STRONG when WRONG** concept will be felt. This strong when wrong concept meaning you will only feel the weight of the world conscience when you are not thinking correct thoughts. A good analogy is a quiet public library where others are talking in a quiet voice; still the people who are concentrating on their studies are not that much interfered with. If the policing by the world conscience interferes with one's thinking even though they are thinking correct thoughts, then this is only temporary as the Flip is programmed to correct itself against negativity.

The universal mind allows for the forming and continual running of the world conscience that takes advantage of transparency of thoughts in the conscious and sometimes thoughts in the pre-conscious for ***ethical policing*.** The world conscience applied with telepathy will be **"STRONG when WRONG"** and really not felt otherwise. There will be many taboo thoughts in the pre-conscious because it is here where they are all turned away from the conscious and pushed back from conscious view. People will be pushing away these thoughts of temptation and this needs to be taken into consideration as some people try to resist bad thoughts as you view them with telepathy in the pre-conscious zone.

If thoughts in the pre-conscious are dwelled on with Flip from another person these pre-conscious thoughts will summate into the conscious and then will receive judgment by all consciouses in proximity now. Care must be taken by all people to refrain from dwelling on bad thoughts if felt in the pre-conscious of others. Generally these pre-conscious thoughts are perceived as too quiet and incomplete by others. "Others" refers to any person other than the ***originator*** of the thought. This summation telepathy scanning by others may also benefit you by helping to repel your own socially incorrect thoughts back into the pre-conscious zone and strengthen your conscious threshold barrier wall against incomplete trash thoughts from the pre-conscious zone.

I would like to add the fact that if a master like myself perceives mal intent in a person's mind then I can highlight the person in the crowd with only psychic energy or even circle the person's head for the police with an image projection. In time others will be able to key in on criminals with telepathy singling them out for the police and the good citizen remaining unidentified, possibly done at a distance. You must also note that if you pursue proficiency with mental telepathy and do bad things you will be **punishing yourself** as you acquire more skills in telepathy because you will make yourself available for more scrutiny as you think deviant thoughts.

All this sounds a little scary to me and probably you as our freedoms will be taken away by Flip transparency but this telepathy always corrects itself to prevent it from being offensive to anyone. So I think everything will work out for the best as the telepathy adjusts as we go along into the future. Another added fact here is that the human being is super communicative and social and telepathy is just a natural innate function to develop these communication and social skills.

Transformation of Already Formed Images

Images already formed in the surrounding environment may be transformed into something else similar by Flip image projection if the general shape is already there. This is a great game for children if one of the adults possesses some ability for telepathy image projection. Sadly to say children often turn to drugs to be imaginative but in the future if a child wants to be imaginative then drugs will not be needed for mind altering rather simple games of telepathy, a nice thought for the future I think.

A cloud or a mountain may be transformed by telepathy projection into various images other than the original obvious perception as long as it is close to the original shape of the object. Planes flying over you may take on the shape of a shark very easily with telepathy transformation.

This all is accomplished with a **simpler and easier form of mental telepathy image projection.** By just adding a couple of fins in your mind along with a mouth and eye and then imagining to push them out from your conscious mind into the shape of the airplane will change it into a shark appearance inside everybody's conscious mind and slightly also appear to be a shark in the outside world too. This is all constructed from your memory of what the shape should look like and then pushed into the original image transforming it with telepathic image projection.

This taking an already existing shape in nature and transforming it by image telepathy is easier to do than totally creating an image of your own from scratch. This image transformation is a great imaginative game to be played by adults and children. This Flip transformation may aid in the forming of a total image projection of your own in the future by practicing this more elementary transformation of images that is easier to do than clear original image projection.

Also things may be highlighted, filled in, or saturated with color just a little more such as a weak colored rainbow or sunset may be enriched to contain darker fuller colors with transformation telepathy, and possible even more with the help of others through telepathy summation.

Psychology with Telepathy

Criminology- The World Trade Center plane attacks in New York City might have been prevented if the terrorists involved were exposed by foot talking or sound Flip by the other passengers waiting in the airport terminal. **These criminal terrorists had to be full of violent energy as well as high emotions of fear inside their minds even though they were calm on the outside as they occupied the airport terminals.**

Violent thinking is highlighted with more psychic energy than any other thought besides love. This violent psychic energy was most definitely perceived by a few people with mental drift (weak unsynchronized telepathy) or clear strong telepathy but nothing was said for fear of being called a sick person with abnormal anxiety if this was vocalized to a security guard and proved not to be true. You must remember that mental telepathy is a newly given fact in the 21st century and not be afraid to voice it when needed in an emergency.

However casually communicating through foot talking or using sound Flip about what you felt about this violence coming from the terrorists' mind would be perfectly accepted and possibly investigated by security guards thereby stopping these terrorists. All the security guards in the airports could be taught to watch for foot talking or sound Flip warnings. Easy mind reading is accomplished if high emotions are present in the conscious or short term memory.

High emotions in a criminal person's conscious may also be artificially induced by intensified questioning at the security check points at the airport, which would cause anxiety and increase emotions that would heighten psychic energy for helping in reading the conscious of the criminals' minds.

Local police enforcement could also use these tools of telepathy for investigating and protecting the public. People in the neighborhood could give information to police with casual foot talking or by passing by the police in a car using the sound Flip of their auto.

Police may form a summation telepathy network of say 5 or more people with one of the individuals in the group being an accomplished telepathist. When a type of sick criminal who calls to taunt the police phones into the police station the summation telepathic ring will all pick up the phone together and all listen quietly for powerful clues leaking from the sociopath's short term memory through the phone. **Remember that a telephone is a powerful auxiliary helping device that makes mind transference or mind reading a lot easier to do especially in a summation telepathy group.** Images or words may be picked up by the police summation group as they listen to the criminal talk on the phone helping to locate and catch the criminal. The summation group may be scattered anywhere in the world as they are connected by telephone in simultaneous summation.

Criminally Insane - A ***non-judgmental friend*** of a criminally insane person may help strengthen moral right and also beef up the conscious threshold barrier not allowing illogical and disorganized thoughts to enter the sick friend's conscious mind from the area of the disoriented and out of touch pre-conscious or primitive mind as they both casually practice ***telepathy summation strengthening*****.** Flip is not offensive to the sociopath's mind over the course of the entire day. This telepathy strengthening may be accomplished by constantly playing music and Flipping a few controlling words and phrases with telepathy into the sound of the music around the mentally handicapped person and in their home. A monitoring close friend should choose words that may help reassure and comfort the sick friend's mind giving confidence and enabling the sociopath's mind to avoid entering paranoia or conscious confusion of what the correct thing is to do. The Flip monitor or teacher holds controlling thoughts in the sociopath's mind with psychic energy that is done through telepathy. A radio type broadcast or subliminal broadcast as described later in this chapter may also be used. An intercom may be connected to the sociopath's house and sound Flip performed with music in the criminal's home or pumped in from a friend's house with live Flip contained.

Insane people are flooded with irrational and illogical thoughts from the pre-cognitive area that may be caused by a weak conscious threshold barrier between the conscious and pre-conscious. This conscious thought barrier wall keeps junk and incomplete pre-conscious thoughts along with primitive mind's wants from entering the conscious. Irrational thoughts heard and seen in the conscious mind need to be corrected by exchanging bad thoughts inside the conscious with good thoughts. Summation telepathy may give strength through psychic energy, which is really just "thinking energy" that will help repel these bad thoughts back into the pre-conscious and keep the conscious mind occupied with other correct thoughts. **At times other people currently plugged into the universal mind by telepathy who are in the sick person's immediate area may help correct bad conscious thoughts with mental telepathy on occasion.** You have to remember that paranoid schizophrenics will sound Flip the entire day with no signs of tiring or offense to their minds'.

A person should over time be able to pick up on his criminally insane friend's mental drift or possible transparency of conscious mind if a lot of time is spent with this particular individual. Sound telepathy will leak conscious thoughts involuntarily from the sick person's mind while music is playing and his friend should pick up on this. It should be noted that a lot of criminally insane people appear to be the nicest people but these individuals possess an irresistible urge to commit terrible deviant acts. Some of the sociopath's deviant episodes bring harm to people and caution should be exercised as the bad thoughts are sure to come around sooner or later and this sick person may act them out.

If a person should dwell on a criminal thought for more than 3 seconds, then this person is mentally ill and needs conscious thought correction. If a person dwells on a thought for more than 3 seconds then generally he or she is putting together a plan for accomplishing this concept and this may become habit forming over time resulting in acting out this scenario. A couple of examples here would be a sick person that has thoughts about having sex with an 8 year old child or possibly a man constructing a real murder in his mind. If these people think these incorrect thoughts for 3 seconds or less then this person is a totally normal person. Our primitive mind has a hard time differentiating the fact that this opposite sex person has to be a certain age and puts pressure on the mind for sex survival thoughts. Physical world senses coming into the conscious mind of a normal person will definitely figure out that this child is too young to have sex with and this should be perceived in 3 seconds or less. All modern socialized people should never dwell more than 3 seconds about primitive sex thoughts or any other criminal thought or they will be considered mentally ill. A person may be exempt from judgement if they are reading a serial killer novel or watching a murder movie on television as for now this seems to be the norm. Although murder movies are good for the general population many violent things should not be allowed to be downloaded into the sociopath's short term memory over a 72 hour period. Care must be taken not to saturate a sociopaths 72 hour memory with violence.

When a handicapped person becomes sick through stress or feels threatened they begin to be out of touch with reality. People around the sick individual can help hold the mentally ill person within the bounds of reality or get the **sick individual realigned with reality through telepathy communication and reinforcement of good thoughts.** Telepathy may not be able to keep all bad thoughts from entering a sociopath's mind but it will definitely help keep them in reality awareness with the world around them with their friends coaching telepathy techniques. **For many**

people reality and the sickness of not knowing what reality is a very fine line and telepathy in many cases will help keep sick people from "going over this line into the area of insanity." This realignment of reality in sick people through telepathy will help cut back on crime and maybe help keep people from getting hurt.

Criminal Dream Suggestion - a criminal may have dream suggestion (see page 66) done to them by a summation group voluntarily or involuntarily. The summation group talking to a sleeping criminal may pick up on clues to solve a crime. The military could interrogate prisoners in much the same way.

Sociopath Thought Transparency and Amplification of Physical World Movements

Computerized groups of neighborhood watch have been monitoring ***sociopaths*** in many big cities in North America as many of these sociopaths are guilty of repeating the same types of crime over and over again. These Sociopath Watches are done 24 hours a day, 7 days a week. Eventually many of these schizophrenic criminals somehow sneak away unnoticed time and time again to commit terrible repeat crimes of rape and murder. These sociopaths repeat their modus operandi over and over again even though they are being monitored 24/7 by neighborhood watches. Neighborhood watch head mothers who volunteered for these monitor programs stated that the **criminals being monitored were practically invisible at times for unknown reasons**.

It is possible that the sociopath's schizophrenic mind is not in touch with the real physical world due to their conscious physical input and conscious selection of thought not functioning when these criminals become sick. This non-functioning conscious makes them not part of the physical tangible dimension for other people to pick up on with their normal senses. This seems to be a type of reflection of the real world through the criminal's conscious mind that at times does not reflect or function correctly in the sociopath due to the conscious becoming sick. It may also be possible that the sociopath's bio-chemical processes in their brain are not reacting properly resulting in low volume conscious thoughts that are unperceivable to others making them somewhat invisible for committing crimes.

Telepathy if taught to the schizophrenic criminal will enable amplification of their physical movements and transparency of their thought for monitoring by other people around them even though their conscious is non-functioning. The telepathy will highlight and amplify all thoughts and physical movement such as opening a window, and also the physical movement of walking away from their monitored home will be connected now to physical world a little better and amplified for neighborhood watch observers. The sociopaths could be taught foot talking or sound Flip that would become habit forming and when practiced give notice to themselves by highlighting their actions.

I would like to relate an incidence that occurred to me while in the military serving as a medic in the mountain patrol located in the German and Austrian Alps. I was a ski patrolman and medic serving temporary duty while skiing the mountain resorts of the Alps caring for military people and their families while on they were on vacation in Europe. One day a large man fell skiing and badly separated his shoulder on the mountain. I assisted the man immobilizing his shoulder and took the man down the mountain by toboggan and loaded him into our truck ambulance. This man was in great pain as some shoulder separations can put forth due to the tearing of large muscles connecting the shoulder. This injured man was out of his head from the pain of his injury and keep talking about his mother baking cookies the whole time while riding to the hospital.

All of the Army medics are trained to keep talking to injured people to prevent the injured person from going into shock and making things worse. Well the ride to hospital from the mountain took about 1 and a half hours to travel and the whole time this man was out of his head talking about his mother and her baking cookies. Well naturally to say after about 45 minutes of talking about his mother baking cookies I got tired of this conversation and I stopped talking to him about his mother; 2 minutes later the man started going into shock. I got the oxygen bottle out, gave him oxygen for a couple of minutes and then continue to talk to the man about baking cookies with his mother all the way to the x-ray table where the doctor took over. As long as I was communicating with this man he could maintain and not think about the pain and stay out of shock preventing a more dangerous situation. I think that if talking was blocked telepathy may serve to communicate reassurances, also **accidents such as banging the wall in a cave in, avalanche, or banging on the bulkhead of a sunken submarine would communicate and alleviate stress.**

Communication keeps a person's mind in reality and telepathy is a form of communication; maybe not as good as vocally talking to a person but it will help in keeping a person's mind healthy.

Group Therapy - A group instructor can read from a script that explains acting out a particular deviant scene or phobia scenario while in a ***telepathy summation group*** that is concentrating with eyes closed focusing on the image scene being read by the instructor. This group may help instill with practice a moral conscience or desensitization of phobias by practicing telepathy imaging while in this summation telepathy group. The group needs to lower all conscious shielding and this lowering of shields is accomplished by the mutual trust and mutual confidence of all people in the group. Without trust and honesty among its members the group will not function and group summation is not possible.

Telepathy summation exerts moral weight on an individual by the total morality rules contained in the living long term memory of the world conscience that the group's telepathy learns to plug into. Numerous group telepathy sessions will begin to instill this correct conscience in their long term physical memory and they will also feel this big brother world conscience constantly watching over them. Over time group therapy will help to correct the thinking of the individuals belonging to this particular work topic group by learning summation telepathy.

Stress Relief - Many problems are attributed to stress, and the basic forms of Flip can help alleviate these stress problems through communication Flip and also **meditation telepathy** as described in its own chapter. If a person is capable of telepathy then the mind will pump its stress thoughts into the universal mind thus reducing stress through the communication of telepathy and also meditation or a combination of both.

Stimulus overload of the short term memory can cause forgetfulness through stress. A person who is cramming for exams or any other concentrated learning task may have problems remembering if their mind becomes too stressed out. Foot talking as you walk downtown or across campus will relieve some of this stress of the mind and help to retain your memorization work.

Nervousness - Pushing telepathy communication out of your internal conscious mind cures nervousness when Flipping say in front of a crowd of people waiting in line at the bank by inserting something in your mind to replace the worry. This Flipping to relieve nervous energy is going to work at various degrees depending on your skill to communicate with people in the immediate vicinity who are presently inside the universal mind (people receiving your pushed out telepathy).

Self-Actualization is the common sense acquired as a person ages but is also taken from the school of Existentialism Psychology. Self-Actualization is the practice of thinking and **choosing** better thoughts as we progress in life. The world conscience with the advent of telepathy exerts moral pressure to help make these right choices helping to choose a more socially correct life for everyone in the world as we learn to feel the moral weight of the world conscience, thus self actualizing.

Emotions - Mental telepathy **amplifies silliness along with violence** and these are emotions have to be reduced as telepathy and age increase. If not corrected this amplification of these emotions will irritate and punish one's self. More thought control is required as a person practices telepathy and grows older. Also note that the emotion of love is amplified and care must also be taken for increased emotions in this area or we will suffer a bleeding aching heart daily.

Aggression - would also be helped by telepathy techniques as Flip allows venting and catharsis.

Radio Subliminal Broadcasts - A live radio broadcast with no time delay spoken by a live person using sound Flip may work to correct or comfort the human mind passively without concentrated listening. Radio waves travel almost exactly the same speed as light; this being approximately 186,000 miles per second. This live radio broadcast will be a synchronized sound Flip throughout the whole world if the broadcast is live and done simultaneously with the broadcaster's sound Flip or with other people assisting. The live sound Flip radio broadcast may contain sound Flipped words that may correct the mind if said over and over by a live person sound Flipping. This live radio broadcast with sound telepathy added may be heard in the prisons by inmates that volunteer for this telepathy live radio program.

A lot of television and radio stations time delay the live broadcast 10 to 15 seconds that is used to cut out bad language with the push of a button when said and this **unsynchronized broadcast** is not unable to be used for live telepathy at this time. **In the near future we may be able to record telepathy but for now it is only a sure thing when the Flip is done live.** The sound or music coming from a pre-recorded radio broadcast may be used for simple sound Flip on the receivers end and this need not be live.

All the telepathy contained in this book will form a separate and new School of Psychology for helping people with problems social and mental.

Psychic Suggestion

Dis-inhitbited with Criminal Intent - If a person is mentally handicapped and temporarily disoriented they may have a social correcting concept inserted in the conscious gallery of their present focus by ***telepathic psychic suggestion.*** Being drunk or influenced by drugs also sometimes leads to the incorrect social behavior and often times criminal behavior; a change in behavior may be accomplished by psychic suggestion. The dis-inhibited person may be reminded of the law and its consequences by psychic suggestion; however psychic suggestion is unable to force the conscious will into compliance due to the conscious will being disabled by the primitive mind's wants.

Telepathic psychic suggestion always possesses a clear thought although possibly being recognized slightly slower than normal when the brain is intoxicated with alcohol or other various types of drugs. The problem with all this nice clear telepathic suggestion is that the **normal will power of the conscious is incapacitated when drugged, drunk, or super tired, which enables the primitive mind to breach the conscious threshold barrier overwhelming the conscious with anti-social desires.**

Although the correct choice is made available through increased awareness of social telepathy for the continuance of your life in a comfortable and law abiding direction, your physically sick or drug altered "conscious will" may possibly ignore this logical advice and choose the wrong response due to other temporary controlling desires. Although psychic suggestion does not control the conscious will, it reduces the ambiguity of a current incorrect situation influencing a correct course of action.

In time the World Conscience will put a stronger pressure on an individual to choose the most socially correct option in a situation of dis-inhibited consciousness. People will feel big brother watching them and experience fear of punishment and guilt from participating in the incorrect behavior for an extended period of time and change this behavior into a socially acceptable one.

Hallucinations

A serious consideration for the reader is to not practice any type of mental telepathy if it bothers your mind. No matter how much fun or ego-inflating this Flip stuff is you do not want to hurt yourself with telepathy. Your increased sensitivity through practicing telepathy could hurt your mind with over stimulation of sense input overloading your conscious. **Remember to always face reality; building a solid foundation as you go forward with mind transference techniques or you will get lost in the woods with no reference point for home in the universe making yourself sick. The truth may be that telepathy is harming your mind and should be totally abandoned.**

Scenarios to consider about yourself when practicing telepathy.

1- Not sick at all, but your ESP ability is making you sick with over stimulation of conscious input and the firing up of space junk thoughts from the pre-conscious that fills your conscious mind incapacitating it.

2- A little sick with a little ESP ability, which also would over stimulate your conscious thinking causing a cluttered mind.

3- Mentally ill with no ESP ability and suffering from hallucinations, audio and visual resulting in false realities.

The 3 listings above have one thing in common, unwanted thought invasion in the conscious focus (over stimulation) that is confusing and sometimes painful. You know you can try ***medicines (drugs)*** to try to remedy your problem of over stimulation. Sometimes drugs are very beneficial in helping your problem and sometimes all you'll get is side effects because they do not help your condition of over stimulation.

Void Meditation Technique is one way to learn to ignore or repel uninvited thoughts coming into your conscious focus. Free your mind from all thought, free it from all images, and free it from all illumination of light. What you want to see is void.

Void is not black, black is a saturated color, which is harder to attain. Void will be hard to describe because we never concentrate on void so there is no color name for void. **The void may appear vague gray black; you'll have to give it a name to help you go there; maybe simply the color void**. This technique of concentrating on void in your conscious gallery teaches the mind to control all incoming thoughts and repel those that are not wanted.

This thought control from meditating will not occur overnight; you will begin to notice some control after about three months, 10 minutes per day. Slowly over more months of practice you will attain more control as you practice your daily meditation. This void technique positively worked for me giving me a lot more control of uninvited thoughts I have at times from other people's telepathy transmissions. Sometimes my conscious mind is flooded with summation telepathy from others that sometimes is simple random energized space debris coming in from my pre-conscious due to telepathy summation from the dwell of others on my pre-conscious junk.

You can imagine how cluttered up my mind becomes with all the telepathy I pick up on as a master psychic. I could see this cluttered mind thing coming about early in the beginning stages of my emerging telepathy so I began preparing myself early in this telepathy game for this over stimulus of my mind from others summation telepathy; many of these episodes being violent attacks.

At times my conscious becomes flooded with telepathic thoughts on occasion when I close my eyes before sleep. I have come to realize this bombardment of telepathic thoughts in my conscious can be controlled with concentration on void and **when I fall asleep my conscious shuts down and at this time of conscious shutdown this bombardment of thoughts ceases to exis**t. You need to tell yourself that this over stimulation will not last long and hang in there until it passes or you fall asleep, and if need be re-open your eyes, which will relieve the over stimulus of uninvited thoughts and this bad time will pass.

As with any disease of the mind the frequency of the episodes must be noted and recorded. If this happens more than twice in one week or continues to happen you might need medical help at least until you can learn some control with void meditation or you might need to use both medicines and meditation to control your thought invasion. I would like to note that sometimes this thought invasion is a little painful for me with my eyes closed before I fall asleep but once familiar with this thought invasion you can learn not to let it rule you.

I would also like to note that sometimes I am heavily bombarded with telepathy from others for various reasons and sometimes due to a sickness (fever, migraine, or worry) I am weak to repel intrusive thoughts away from my conscious. I have however adapted and expect to continue to adapt and grow stronger against thought invasion due to telepathy over stimulus from others. I do not use drugs but if I needed meditation I would not hesitate to use these drugs if need be.

Anxiety will result from thought invasion and over stimulus due to practicing telepathy, just become familiar with it and do not be overly afraid of 20 or 30 minute bouts on occasion and stay strong. After you have dealt with these thought invasion telepathy thoughts meanwhile practicing the void meditation technique you will begin to realize you have the ability to constantly win out over these thoughts and your confidence builds lessening the anxiety of these over stimulus events.

Please note that I have projected over 10,000 telepathic images to date and I have really never had any hallucinations of images. I receive images of telepathy that are unwanted thought invasion from other people (normally with my eyes closed) but these are not hallucinations and not out of touch reality sequences. At times I also receive space junk in my conscious focus from my pre-conscious that has been highlighted by other people's telepathy. At times incomplete thoughts from my pre-cognitive area flood my conscious mind due to telepathy focus of other people or a breakdown in my conscious threshold barrier due to sickness, extreme worry, or strong fatigue.

Have no fear; if you are a true psychic you will just have to face reality so you can maintain good mental health or improve your sick condition. Psychics have to believe in logic and truth or mastering telepathy will not be possible. If mental telepathy bothers your mind, simply leave it alone in this world; it is not your job or requirement to practice mind transference on planet earth if it bothers your mind even if you are Psychic. This means never lying to yourself about anything preventing mental illness from occurring or getting worse.

Here is a test to try if you hear voices in your head with no physical person around. Fountains with flowing water or waterfalls give off all kinds of voices to all people to different degrees as you practice mind transference listening. As you listen for Flip from fountains of flowing water or waterfalls they seem to begin to talk as if they have holy voices of instruction from God coming from the flowing water. These voices are obviously junk with absolutely no basis, space debris floating through the pre-conscious universe with no bearing on anything at all. They sound great but they are for entertainment purposes only. These voices of instruction could be incomplete thoughts from the short term memory or preconscious illogical thought, who knows, they are junk voices never to be taken seriously. **These voices I am describing from the flowing water or waterfalls are a type of auditory hallucination**. Remember not to "listen" for vague telepathy, real telepathy is clearer and has a more directed focus.

Now compare your voices in your head with the fountain or waterfall voices, are they the same? **Also, keep a journal of your irritating thoughts to see if they show a train of thought** that may really be a form of communication coming from anywhere in the universe or write them off as just space junk highlighted with telepathy from others with no reason just floating haphazardly through the universe.

Being a psychic you will always hear space junk at times and you should simply just turn down the volume ignoring this space junk through the acquiring of mind control techniques.

Keep in mind that a master telepathist can project a type of auditory or visual hallucination but this is a more clear form of communication. In a short time, a matter of minutes, you should be able to tell the difference between false telepathy (visual hallucinations) and real image telepathy and also false sound hallucinations when compared to sound Flip.

The idea for this chapter on Hallucinations came from my former internet web site that I ran on the internet for 4 years. I had received dozens of inquiries about thought invasion through this web site that contained a synopsis of this book Flip. By the way the Flipmt.com website was number one in the world when it was up and running for two years. So I found myself answering many questions about telepathy summation of pre-conscious thoughts or simple random telepathy transmissions crowding the conscious or possible a condition relating to mental illness.

Mental telepathy is a tool of the mind that increases sensory and thought perception and therefore more information is picked up and forwarded into the conscious focus. At times this increase in perception will overload the conscious and anxiety will occur along with possibly a little mental pain.

In this chapter I try to explain the differences between mental illness and telepathy over stimulus and also ways to control this problem of a crowded conscious with unwanted thoughts. Telepathy may pose a problem for some people and this problem may be an involuntary one that they are incapable of just walking away from. The telepathy however is not evil nor does it continue on a course of negativity; it will always correct itself so be sure to practice mind control and hang in there.

Do not be afraid to seek professional help if need be but remain flexible because telepathy at the time of this writing is considered impossible and the doctor might not benefit you if you say you are telepathic. Special powers such as telepathy are considered by psychologists as a characteristic of a paranoid schizophrenic with visions of grandeur and stating the truth of your telepathic ability may only bring you criticism and harm. I think the telepathy I have discovered is 5000 years ahead of its time presently in the year 2009 so we must take care and thank our lucky stars and venture forward in this cynical world cautiously.

Projection of Images and Symbols

Pure Flip leads us into the next advanced stage of mental telepathy and possibly its highest form, image projection. Telepathic images are prepared and fabricated in the internal conscious mind, then pushed out with pinpoint accuracy to either the ***internal conscious viewing screens*** or the ***outside environment***; both areas being able to be viewed by many other people at the same time and possibly at times the entire universal mind. Medium concentration is needed for image projection, if you teach yourself a strained concentrated technique this might work a little better in the beginning but in the long run you will cut yourself short of more skills by over concentrating.

I would like to point out that these telepathy image projections are faint when compared to the real physical thing but they are fully recognizable by another person receiving them as the intended concept that was imagined in the conscious mind of the transmitter or seen in the outside world. As said before the inner mind's gallery is more lifelike but on a smaller scale than the outside world.

These telepathic images may be viewed inside the gallery of the transmitter's own conscious mind by many other people similar to a television screen in the interior of the transmitter's mind but with a little more 3-dimensional look to it. The **images may be pushed into another person's conscious mind's gallery** other than the originator; and **images may also be projected to the outside physical world.** The images projected onto the inner viewing screens of the conscious mind appear small in the interior of the mind when compared to outside images that a person projects into the outside environment. The inner conscious mind fabricates and pushes large images of infinite proportions to the outside world when so desired.

Although the **inner mind's conscious imagery appears to be on a smaller scale** than the outside physical world's screen it is capable in certain form to be more lifelike and a little clearer inside the inner mind than the outside world's screen.

Internal telepathy projections flashed inside the transmitter's conscious mind and intended for others to view are generally received by most people in the surrounding area (approximately 500 meter radius). These internal telepathy projections viewed in the conscious mind of a master Flipper are sometimes transmitted outward without the intent of the master telepathist through ***transparency.***

The outside environment may be entirely the area where your mind's concept begins to form as you create the image concept in the outside world. A person may develop a concept in their interior dimensional gallery of their conscious mind first and then later push it out into the outside environment but it is not necessary to begin internally and everything to do with the concept may develop on the external world screen if desired.

The master telepath's mind is made transparent over time automatically and this enables other people to eavesdrop and view and hear his conscious mind in the immediate area or farther. This telepathy may go thousands of miles with family or close acquaintances who are aware of the master and have a lot of training with him or her in particular; and even at times the entire universe if the receivers are keyed in on the transmitter's mind. If people do not key in on the master telepathist's mind then the people in a 500 meter radius will not know the identity of the transmitter. The master telepathist images and other thoughts are all perceived yet no one can be sure where they originate from but over time or in small groups this will be easily figured out. **It is possible to scare someone's mind really bad with Flip images if this person is not aware of the possibility of Flip.** When aware of Flip projections a person can differentiate between sicknesses and Flip very easily and is less startled.

I am able to project images inside my FM radio for a kilometer or more being viewed by others inside their own FM radio within this radius. I can also project an image in a television set being viewed inside all other televisions within a 1000 meter radius or more. With some people that are familiar with me I can be received a lot farther inside these ***auxiliary devices***. Remember that telephones, radios, televisions are helpers that make telepathy a lot easier to do providing physical synchronized energy and **sometimes auxiliary helpers only aid in giving confidence fooling the mind into accomplishing telepathy.**

Image projection began to take shape almost two years after Foot Talking was initiated (April 1998); image Flipping starting around the spring of the year 2000. I first started mentally projecting simple arrow images approximately 500 meters to the front of my semi-truck pointing to vehicles ahead of me on the highway. I want to point out that I was a professional truck driver and a lot of experimentation and validation has come from this arena of cross-country truck driving coast to coast using everybody on the highway as validation for the telepathy techniques. Everybody on the highway was more than happy to play these games of telepathy with me. These line arrows at first were crude and about the same size as the vehicle at the distance of 500 meters. These arrows appeared to be touching the vehicle in the same area of **present physical space as the vehicle.** This touching of the vehicle is referring to the **proper depth perception placement of the arrow projection.**

A few days later, after first projecting the arrows I discovered that we could also project word captions above vehicles on the highway in the same fashion as the arrows. Later on this caption thing would progress to mental telepathy projection typing appearing to be on a regular white paper page, white marker board, or a computer monitor inside everyone's mind and prove quite readable.

Depth perception placement in the outside world is very important; otherwise the projection would just appear to be on your own windshield in front of your face instead of 500 meters down the road where you intended it. When projecting inside another person's mind it is better to make it fit (compress it) otherwise it runs out the side of their head, which is neither here nor there but it makes for better control to make it fit inside imaginary borders when you can. I usually write words on the outside of my imagined image of a contoured cerebrum and sometimes on the middle of a person's back, these are just a couple of funny habits I enjoy but as for your Flip image you need to suit yourself. It takes a little bit of imagination to place the projection anywhere from in your mind or in another person's mind to infinity but with a little bit of practice you can place the image over 20 miles (extent of the horizon).

Note: the people around you will quickly pick up on the image you projected 20 miles out but most people at the other side of the 20 miles would not notice this Flip unless they were trained with you or were close family or friends of yours, or were looking for this particular image Flip at this same time. If you keyed in on a particular person on an ocean cruise ship on the horizon or something similar then your friend would pick up on your telepathy 20 miles away as you could visually see the ocean liner on the 20 mile ocean horizon in the distance.

Trying to imagine where to place the image projection is a little difficult to achieve. Reference points in the sky (clouds) or ground reference points out to the horizon (mountains, buildings, erections), help place the image projection in its proper depth perception in the outside physical world's field of view. In the far distance it is easier to come up behind the spot intended for the projection and then pull the telepathic image point forward to touch your physical reference point.

Example: Pull an imaginary point up from the earth's horizon to a point behind a cloud in the sky and then bring this point forward slightly to the desired insertion point for the image, possible right in front of the cloud or placed on the particular cloud itself. Now you should feel your imaginary reference point and then project your telepathic image at this point now. Coming up from behind buildings or other types of erections and then placing the projection upon these buildings also works great for depth perception placement. You may also if you wish to project directly on this reference point, whichever seems to work best for you.

Depth perception parameters do different things to the image projection qualities. For example; the mountains in the Western United States have been the site of some of my large image projections on or against the mountains and are quite thrilling such as a giant wolf or deer. On the other hand a jungle trail with a closed overhead tree canopy of say 6 meters of height in Costa Rica, Central America with the appearance of a leaf tunnel has also offered some fantastic looking image projections. This smaller scale of the jungle trail has made for some beautiful images such as a 2 meter dragonfly projected 20 meters ahead on the jungle path, awesome and detailed in a different setting of closed depth perception.

Many thousands of images, (at the time of this 2009 writing approximately ten thousand images) along with foot talking, pure, emotions and various other forms of mental telepathy had to be validated before I could confidently write about them and explain the techniques. Pure forms of mental telepathy, image Flipping, and sound telepathy were mainly validated on the highway as a truck-driver where as foot talking was validated anywhere walking around people.

You can imagine how I felt when people first started to perceive these images I was Flipping on the highway; I was truly astounded the same as you the reader would be. It took 2 or 3 days of projecting images and being validated vocally by others before I could really believe this was occurring. I had just finished the 2nd revision of my manuscript of this Book Flip and I wanted to take a break from all this telepathy stuff. I was thinking maybe a couple of months to be free of this monster called Flip along with the burden of writing as I was working long hours driving truck and the writing was hard to explain. So now I began Flipping images and taking notes again for a 3rd revision and there never ever was a break from this Flip writing. I would like everyone to take note that I am a better writer now and enjoy it more so than in the beginning but I also have more time to do so now.

So began the chapter on image projection and the sought after vacation from Flip was over before it started. Kind of a hilarious situation occurring here being that this new telepathy gift of mine never seemed to stop growing in power. Almost like the powers of the universe wanted to roll forward with no stopping. To me it was like when is this fantastic stuff ever going to stop progressing? With image Flipping I just knew we were on our way to the stars and back instantly with telepathy. It was beyond belief that in a time period of a little over 2 years we had progressed so far, so fast.

This is one of the reasons for this book to explain how far we have taken Flip Telepathy, record it, and hopefully this book will hold us firmly in the reality of the progress we so far achieved in mental telepathy.

I know how ridiculous and unbelievable all this image Flipping must sound to you the reader. You must know that however fantastic all this image Flip and other forms of telepathy are, it is my obligation to tell the world the truth. I truly believe telepathy is the cure for the universe and the God's or God of the universe dictate I relate the truth about telepathy to you.

In the outside physical world the ***further you project*** your telepathic image, the ***greater the size***, the more ***detail,*** the amount of ***color saturation or contrast***, the brighter ***illumination,*** and the placement of ***depth perception*** are the factors that determine the difficulty of the image projection. Images that a person projects may be small or large, viewed internally in the conscious mind or pushed out into the physical world as I mentioned before. These projections are from the size of a dime or smaller to filling the entire sky above you.

I like to Flip the HOLLYWOOD sign because it is large and well memorized by myself and other people. Ordinarily this long sign would be very difficult for me but the sign has been well memorized by myself and others from the sight of it so many times in the media. **Being well memorized makes the left to right scan of your**

projection easier to do especially if the word is long. We print left to right in the western world but it is just as easy to project the Flip image right to left.

When spelling a word in a telepathic projection pushed to the outside world you may push one letter of your word out at a time by holding it there with your memory and then continue to write and complete the image. Remember you have approximately 3 seconds to complete your image when first beginning in Flip imagery. It is possible to Flip project the entire image completely all at once and this method may be better for you. With my past telepathic experience I have found it an easier scanning or spelling the image by holding the first part of the Flip image in place by memory and then continuing to add or spell the word.

It is possible that long words or complicated images necessitate scanning in the outside world because of the size and also this scanning movement possible creates the illusion of more light tricking the mind, allowing more detailed telepathy.

Images projected out into the night sky are a little more difficult to give the impression of illumination and detail but nighttime Flips or low light images are some of the most impressive. A person who is projecting a Flip at night may imagine lighting the image with a separate image of external lighting produced by your imagination right along with the Flipped image making for two merged images into one. **Black lettering projected on the dark background of night has almost no contrast but is very easy to do.** Naturally black on black does not compare to an illuminated Flip image at night but it is still readily perceived and much easier to do.

When Flipping some images in the outside physical world especially lettering, contrast is hard to produce clearly. When image Flipping lettering at night, black on black is readable however illuminated white on a night black sky is a lot better although the more contrast and illumination added the more difficult it becomes and the more concentration is needed.

In the daytime sky white lettering on blue sky is the most effective and fairly easy to do. You may extract the color white from a cloud same as a painter's palette and then block letter in this matching white color next to the cloud that is the source of your white color. Letters Flipped in the sky may have a three dimensional effect rocking back and forth as if ready to fall from supports, then falling from the sky making crashing sound Flips as they hit the earth. 3-D images are hard to imagine and are best accomplished with movement such as a shark swimming through the sky. If the object is large it is hard to rapidly scan the entire picture to maintain an impression of a single frame Flipped at once. A person can fill the entire sky with a mental telepathy projection; however this scenario is very hard and should be well memorized.

An easy telepathy projection to do is finger painting by covering an imaginary sheet of glass with a saturated color of paint or a paper substance having a white substrate. Scraping the paint off the imaginary sheet of glass paper will expose the etched letters, or scraping the paint off the paper exposing the white substrate underneath making simple shapes such as a triangle, square, circle, an X or possible just a simple line or scratch.

Simple fruit shapes are easy and produce clear image projections such as an orange, apple, or banana. An imaginary sheet of glass with a white paint happy face is very easy to do and another favorite of mind is a painted hand pressed on the imaginative glass surface. An imagined glass surface may be totally painted and then a person can imagine scraping off the dry painted surface exposing simple line silhouette designs.

When something in the outside physical world is focused on with simple telepathy or when an image is inserted with Flip projection it sticks out very prominently.

One example is a small single clump of grass, Flip projected as an image in the distance in the dimension of the outside world that will stick out tremendously even though the projection is the same color green as the surrounding grass. A naturally occurring clump of grass may also be keyed upon solely with simple telepathy focus and all people in a radius for 500 meters will also know that this particular clump of grass is the one you are focusing on.

An extra star may be inserted as a projected Flip in the night sky full of thousands of similar stars and all the people around you will notice your extra inserted star with image Flip. A single star may also be highlighted with simple telepathy concentration (focusing on one single star) or a small projected circle drawn around the star. With all the thousands of stars in the sky around your Flipped image of a star or by highlighting a single star in the Milky Way band with solely telepathic concentration, the mental projection will be recognized by everyone as the star you inserted or highlighted.

This unique quality about stars being singled out of the entire sky makes me hope my theory of reaching the stars with Flip holds true. **It seems that if everybody on earth can tell which star I singled out with telepathy then it is logical that intelligent life in the star area should also know that we are communicating with it. Telepathy's psychic energy does not have to obey physical law and this should be easy to do with Flip.** If addressed correctly by familiarity and known location telepathy concepts will be able travel the entire universe.

Colors may be added to images and are only slightly more difficult than black and white requiring a little more memorization for the coloring of the picture with Flip. More than two colors is extremely difficult to image project. I sometimes take a giant bucket of paint of one color such as red paint and spill it out into a large portion of the sky. This is fairly easy and has good effect for all that view it but again it is only a single color.

Images may be of three different types all a little different in appearance. **Images**

may appear to be *drawn*, *real life type*, and the *motion picture type*, all capable of having movement, sound, emotion, touch, taste and smell added to the projection. Any more than two senses attached to the Flip image would prove most difficult for a single person; however complex images with many senses attached could be accomplished by a group of people summating telepathy images together by different members adding different pieces.

Duration of the telepathic image projection for me is about 3 seconds in length. For me the image normally begins to fades in and out after 3 seconds and then dissipates. If the image is complicated a brief rest to recharge the image is required of one to two minutes or possibly more time if the image was straining. You should not think of the image while resting. If you give the image a recharge time it will be Flipped again with clarity where if you Flip right away the image will be lacking clarity. A person can Flip two, three, or four images rapidly in a row as long as they are different pictures and you take a couple minutes of recharge before Flipping another series of the same images. A person does not have to wait any length of time if the image you are projecting is very basic and simple such as a white circle. This white circle has no detail or fancy color and can be Flipped every few seconds. An x in black or white would be another example of simple image Flip that needs no rest to recharge.

Let me point out that **I cannot imagine 100% saturation of an imagined projection** in my mind to Flip. The image is a little vague that I see in my mind. **When the image is pushed out from my conscious gallery and projected into the outside environment it is always perceived by others as I had intended yet the image is far from perfect.** The receiver of Flip image will perceive any object familiar or unfamiliar as long as the Flip sender has a fairly well memorized picture or the proper memorized cognitive symbols in their mind to push out.

If the Flip image is weak from the sender, the receiver's memory will add what it can to make a more complete picture for both to identify. In other words the two minds form a third workplace and sometimes both minds working together in this ***3rd*** **area** will arrive at the complete picture or sound which neither could produce by themselves; this again is called ***summation telepathy*.**

If you were to look at the full moon and then rapidly project the image of the moon with mental telepathy it would not be 100% saturated in color and detail yet everyone would recognize the image as the full moon. Over time I have developed the ability to project images with less and less saturation and detail and still be totally recognized as the intended projected concept. I guess everybody gets better at this stuff with practice and you require less concentration and added detail for recognition of the image projections over time.

Image Flipping with cursive writing is easy and can be drawn with a giant crayon in the sky or on a white regular writing size tablet in another person's hands. You can imagine taking the drawing device in your hand moving it along or you can write only using your mind. **If you use your own imagined hand in image Flip others will manipulate it and it is human nature to do so in a destructive way.** This why it is better to use your mind to produce and move the drawing pen and not your hand in Flip images because people in the crowd always grab your imagined hand and try to manipulate it. **Other people can sometimes contribute their imagined view to your concept of your Flip image altering it a bit or may even strike at your image destroying parts of it.**

Even if a person cannot Flip his or her own image projections they are still capable of altering other people's Flip images or mine. If the image is quick say one-second of duration there is no way other people have time to alter your Flip images. Mental Telepathy images are really the only Flip of mine that people can alter. Although people often times are destructive toward your image, many times they co-operate and enhance the image creating a beautiful striking image. The pieces you leave out of your image Flip others in a **non-formal summation group** you have simply encountered in public may fill in the image with more color and detail. **This casual public summation group may also hold the image in place for a slightly longer time for you,** perhaps another two seconds to work with resulting in an increase in time of 5 seconds. At times these public group participations will produce beautiful results through summation Flip as they add more detail to your image Flip. In a more planned and structured summation group even better results may be accomplished on a more frequent basis. **If violence is perceived during the image Flip all telepathy will shut down and the image lost.**

Teaching Images - Preschoolers pick right up on the telepathy image projections like a fish to water. I was walking by a couple of pre-schools and Flipped a projection of a teddy bear and all the children were yelling teddy bear. Much to my surprise all the children in the pre-school were not afraid and immediately identified the projections and were ready to learn and work with images.

One method for teaching images is to imagine bouncing a ball back and forth slowly or hitting a ball much like a tennis ball between two people. One of the two people involved in this Flip tennis game must be an experienced practitioner of telepathy in order for this to work and teach the beginner to learn to image project the ball.

Another image learning game is the simple computer ping-pong where you hit the ball image back and forth as in a regular match of ping-pong like the old video games. This could be done with the eyes open or closed projecting the game in the inner mind's conscious gallery or projecting it out into the outside natural environment. Sometimes sound added to the bouncing ball such as a bouncing sound of a basketball or tennis ball seems to enhance the image's perception.

Projecting a Stick Man character is a very easy image to do. You first choose a single color and then project a simple stickman composed entirely of lines only, this is for its simplicity of creation through memory. Color is easy to add to the stickman and he can be a bright blue, red, or other memorized color or simply entirely black or white. As mentioned before, triangles, circles, X's, or even a simple line (I) may be drawn very easily.

An image exercise for the internal conscious mind with the eyes shut is using colors that sometimes appear automatically at random in your conscious mind after looking at various sources of outside light not necessarily bright lights. Sometimes with your eyes closed you may see a small spot of light inside your mind. Where the light originates from is not important we just want to use it in our conscious mind for expansion of colors. The colors may be faint and small and at other times fairly bright and large being saturated with color in your mind. When you see a random color come into your conscious with your eyes closed you should begin to concentrate on this color and then expand its size with more concentration and enrich the color saturation more from your memory.

A trick to help you is to imagine pulling a sheet of colored school construction paper into your mind from a past memorized sheet color. You will try to achieve this color from memory by matching and adjusting your original internal spot color to this imaginary color sheet from your memory together in your conscious gallery. With practice you will be able to expand this color and enrich it to fill your whole conscious mind's gallery and sometimes as you build these colors some other dimensional windows will open in your mind due to this conscious mental concentration exercise.

I am always able to expand and enrich colors inside my mind; but it is only on occasion that I am able to open other dimensional windows for viewing with this concentration exercise. This internal color expansion and enrichment is the only time I am in a super concentration mode with mental telepathy. As I mentioned before intense concentration is not good and is counterproductive most of the time with telepathy; medium concentration being the best for practicing Flip. This color expansion exercise with the eyes closed is also a great exercise for mind control against unwanted thought invasion. These windows from other dimensions that open inside your conscious mind at times for viewing are so cool and life like you will be truly impressed. This color exercise may help to learn to push color projections out of your conscious mind into the physical environment.

Simple math problems may be drawn in the sky or internalized on a smaller scale inside your conscious mind or even on an **imaginary school chalkboard.** Old-fashioned **real life black chalkboards** work great for projecting telepathic imaging upon as do **real life white marker boards** in the outside world or imagined inside your mind's conscious gallery.

For me this **imagined simple white marker board** with black marker writing on it is one of the easiest Flip projections to do because of the simple contrast of black on white. A blank, white drive-in movie screen imagined in your mind or in real life works great for Flip too. A person could practice at a blank white drive-in movie screen, film theater screen, or possibly teaching from projecting onto the blank movie screens. Take note the difference here in all these examples being that the screens or projection **boards may be imagined inside your conscious gallery or projected on to the real life boards or screens in the normal outside physical world.**

Another technique of Flipping images is to fabricate them in memory and then push them out into the outside world as quickly as possible coming out of water in some lake or breaking through the ground's surface. Water dripping off the image projection or earth falling away gives the Flip image some sort of depth perception and possible this movement enables the illusion of more light to be added to the image, or possibly just a simple unexplainable trick for improving the image.

Past areas that you have recently viewed, (within a few seconds), may have a Flip image placed there even if they are no longer in view. **<u>You image Flip into a</u>**

<u>previous viewed area from your memory</u>. This past viewed image Flip may not be as strong as present view Flips. For example a car goes by you on the highway and you memorize the vehicles windshield. You then image Flip on the windshield after the car goes by you a few seconds later not looking at the car as you project it doing all this from memory now. It is generally a little weaker than if you were presently viewing the area and as distance increases usually the Flip begins to decrease in strength.

One of the peculiarities of telepathy image projection is when **<u>Flipped by a mirror of any kind say a rearview mirror it always is projected and received readable not reverse like a mirror should be, this must be an indication of something but it baffles me</u>.** There is a possibility that this is an indication that the telepathy is all occurring in the internal conscious mind and not really being projected out to the physical external world at all and instant adjustments are made inside the internal conscious galleries going conscious to conscious.

It is also noted that over time some of the more complex projected Flip images begin to become a little more difficult to produce with use. I am probably talking a hundred or more times with the same image Flip. These memorized projections begin to wear out and are not as sharp as they once were. Possibly due to different variations each time or the addition each time of other people's interpretation of the vision that sometimes enter in a little and alter your image Flip. Perhaps if you quit this particular image for a couple of months doing some re-memorization work and then went back to it, it might then be clear again when Flip projected.

The mental projection visions wear out a little over time; yet popular songs that are repetitive sound Flip just keep getting better. There is less interpretation in cognitive symbols by you and others than pictures resulting in less variation over time.

I am a master Flipper and no intelligent mind on planet earth can refuse one of my thoughts or images, for now anyway. **So my thoughts when really "pushed" on someone are intrusive and unstoppable each and every time I Flip.** Most of the people at the time of this writing do not mind me entering their mind because they are curious and enjoy this new toy called Flip. As long as you practice ethics when Flipping images into other people's conscious mind it probably will not be too much of a problem when being perceived by them and not really incapacitating to an individual who receives normal nice Flip thoughts.

Some of my normal internal spoken thoughts and images leak to the outside environment without the conscious push-out of telepathy transmission and are picked up by everyone around me, however no one really knows where these thoughts originated unless I identify myself. My friends and other people I have trained will just guess that it is me simply because they know my mind's memory and I am the only master Flipper communicating with my particular friends at this time.

However if my thoughts or any other person's thoughts are violent in nature or have high emotional energy these thoughts or images will then possess a lot of psychic recognition power and will be almost impossible to hide and conceal my identity. This hiding of a person's violent thoughts may be possible only for a few minutes; it is that tough to maintain control over these violent or high charged emotional thoughts and of course with violent thoughts your identity is immediately made known.

Image Validation - When a person begins to do mental telepathy projections he or she will have to receive positive verification that they are actually Flipping these images. Validation in the form of returned vocalized repetition of what the transmitted image concept was by another person is best although return validation may be in the form of foot talking, sound Flip, or any of the other forms of telepathy.

One type of positive identification that you are actually image Flipping is digital time (9:30); this image is Flipped at exactly the present time (although the digital numbers not indicating your present correct time), this image of digital time chosen to project by you at random. For example you image Flip 9:30 at 10:00 and somebody will validate that this is the wrong time, but a correct validated image for you. Rush hour traffic is a good place to Flip images and receive validation that you are really doing telepathic projections by listening for a **voice response** and usually there are many in heavy traffic because **people enjoy playing this Flip game in traffic and are**

dis-inhibited here due to anonymity of many cars.

Normally when you image Flip a word the sound Flip of the word is automatically attached and this confuses the validity of the image Flip by the possibility of it being a Pure Flip (with internal spoken thought sent as sound and not an image Flip. This all necessitates validation tricks to rule out these variables.

Exact locations in the sky, abbreviations or punctuation added to word images are some of the tricks to make a response that **rules out variables**. A good image Flip is the abbreviation **H2O** and simultaneously attaching the sound Flip of the word **water**. Someone in a large crowd of people will yell; **"Hey that was an H2O word image not the word water" it never fails;** this trick rules out variables of sound Flip interference and is helpful for the confidence of your mind. Letters may be slightly different at the end of the **word image Flip** by size, curving down, omitting one letter that would misspell the word, curve the word to an arch shape, or angle the word up.

Word projections may have motion much like a computer saver screen spinning and changing size. Words may be drawn; or a word may have two colors in it. The type of image might be cartoon or real life.

A person needs a gimmick for reassurance that they actually performing Flip image and there are many types and they all work to give confidence to your mind making your image Flip stronger by ruling out variables.

Three-dimensional Flipping is possible and I have done it so well that it amazed even me, however this type of internal mind projection happened to me only 2 or 3 times and hardly ever happens when attempted on conscious demand. It is a great thing to be able to do and view as the pictures viewed are totally real life and moving. One time I was able to push a clear image from my conscious of a green 1-meter phosphorescent crescent in 3-D Hologram to a distance of 4 meters for 5 seconds but this was just a fluke so far.

It might be easier for these enriched real life projections to be accomplished by a summation group. **In group summation telepathy the groups' single mind will be able to see all sides at once of an object viewed including hidden views and this may in time be learned by the human mind to view an object with a total surround view.**

In time children that are raised with Flip will be able to have clearer images with telepathy but for us old timers to take on this new reality and develop it extensively, it is going to be extremely hard. Like I said; I have done three-dimensional real life projections but not many and not on command and all but one of these in the interior of my mind.

After a person gets good at telepathic image projection they become disenchanted a bit. The magic wears off because you want more from your images in form of a real life three-dimensional look along with the movement of real life images. So after projecting many images that are totally perceived in everyone's conscious mind but not as clear as the sender would like, your mind begins to be frustrated. You will always want to conjure up a clearer and sharper images improving them and striving towards perfection. You will become bored and frustrated even though you are doing the impossible and are perfectly understood every time you image project. This is a natural self-improvement wish that may never come true for us in our lifetime or may only happen once in a great while.

I myself am not capable of sustaining a clear mental telepathy projection for more than 3 seconds. This limit of only a few seconds of image might be a protective device of the mind to keep from having compulsive images play over and over again jamming the conscious mind. The conscious mind has to be capable of releasing thoughts or images to make room for the next thought to be focused on. I think in time other people will come forward that can hold mental telepathy images for a sustained duration with practice.

I do believe if I saw the Space Shuttle at night as a moving illuminated satellite circling the earth (due to the reflection of sunlight) I could image Flip the astronauts inside the Space Shuttle in orbit at night. This should be simple to do because I know mankind has ventured into space many times and this serves as a known reference point for my mind giving it confidence making this Flip easy to do. Another fact here is if I can see any object, I can pure Flip or image Flip it very easily no matter what the distance.

A mind that is capable of sustaining images could perceive mental telepathy from a far away galaxy and actually walk the far away planet along with the person sending the mental telepathy scenes from this far away galaxy; sustaining mental projections would make this easily possible.

If it is not possible for one person to sustain telepathic image projections then I think that a summation group of individuals could hold the telepathic image in their conscious mind's gallery for the group to work with. Why go to a far away galaxy when you can experience it in the comfort of your living room through mental telepathy.

Telepathy is the ultimate in space travel; eventually able to pick up on all six senses sent by mental telepathy from a place in space billions of light years away all instantly.

I truly believe mental telepathy will occur instantly along with return transmissions anywhere in the universe no matter how far away without a time delay as Flip ignores physical rules of time and energy inside our mind. **Our ultimate goals of mankind and space travel will be accomplished with pure thought telepathy carried in a simple, humble, human mind with no machine ever needed.**

Image Summation will produce a clear detailed and saturated picture for problem solving in the future with a trained group of individuals. The difficulty may be holding the image for extended periods of time along with the details of the concept for problem solving. **If the image should begin to fade other people in the group will share the thought and hold the image intact and in clear focus. In order for this image summation to continue concentration must be maintained through trust and interference has to be controlled, such as violence.**

Some gifted people such as a chess player that can play blind folded would be capable of sustaining many three-dimensional telepathic concepts for a longer period. I myself am not capable of sustaining an image for over three seconds alone presently.

Images never seen before by mankind will be possible in the near future. A said before a summation group will view these telepathic images three-dimensional with an added view of the hidden side shared within the group. One individual of the group may view the backside of the object and meld this backside-hidden view into the summation image of the total group.

Experiments in Illumination

Total darkness is needed for a telepathy illumination experiment to take place; over perhaps a period of four or five days. Physical world illumination is received by the conscious physical input area and some of this illumination is then pumped into the short term memory and stored there. The experimental time period we are talking about here must be void of this illumination for more than 72 hours, which is about the limit of the short term memory thereby ruling out the short term memory's illumination or re-illumination abilities for telepathy. This would then require the long term memory to create telepathic projected illuminated images from stored light over a greater period from the long term memory source. These experiments would all help prove the illumination characteristics of the human mind and possibly teach image projection.

Upon wakening in the morning a person takes in the day's first sunlight for a couple of minutes through his or her conscious sense of sight. Now it is possible for a person to close their eyes and then again reproduce from memory the first morning burn on their conscious gallery screen that is a fresh and uncontaminated screen at this point. The first morning burn of sunlight is so intense that it will sometimes produce light again from your short term memory with your eyes closed. A person may visualize this light again in his or her conscious gallery with their eyes closed sometimes with tremendous results. Short term memory seems to store first morning light with intensity for 3-5 minutes.

Generally a person's viewing of first morning light just burns the *eye retinas*, which is another physical sequence that may be used for illumination control exercises in the internal mind. Normally if a bright light is viewed in the early morning upon awakening or at any other time colors will appear when you immediately close your eyes. Colors such as red or green will appear in your conscious coming from previous viewed light that has temporary imprinted your **eye's retinas**.

As said in the Meditation chapter these colors may be concentrated on and enlarged to fill your entire conscious. With your eyes closed concentrating on this particular available color in your conscious will on occasion open your internal mind's other dimensional doors for 3 dimensional viewing. Be advised that bright color does not have to be stared at for any length of time as these bright lights are a normal daily occurrence.

Short term memory probably stores sunlight for a 72-hour period. Not having stored sunlight in your short term memory probably contributes to depression from lack of this stored sunlight.

Ethics

The transmission of radio signals and television signals are many times delayed for 5 to 10 seconds, this time delay used to initiate censorship of spoken verbal thought. Mental Telepathy is heard as internal spoken thought; should it also be allowed a politeness delay of 5 to 10 seconds for censorship of bad or unintentional thoughts? Once mental telepathy summation focuses on a **shared thought** in the pre-conscious zone it begins to be noticed but still may be ignored at this point by the consciouses of two or more people. **A shared telepathy thought becomes etched in stone or breaks threshold into the conscious for vivid recognition when it is continued to be focused on for more than 3 seconds or when someone vocalizes this thought with a normal voice.** This continued focus of more than 3 seconds on another person's thoughts or "dwell" is normally going to be considered unethical unless a need for help or warning is needed.

Once *pure Flip* is learned or if you even practice *foot talking* and *sound Flip* long enough, the brain will on occasion leak out a few thoughts and some of your conscious thoughts will become readable to people around you in the vicinity of say 100 meters. A few words of thought will inadvertently leak at times into your footsteps and also through the sounds around you by sound telepathy. An example of accidental thought slippage by telepathy would be washing dishes resulting in the splashing water sounds or clashing of the dishes that would pull thoughts from your mind. Being ***dis-inhibited*** (drunk, drugged, or tired) will increase the likelihood of leaking these normally hidden thoughts from your conscious mind into the unintentional Flip techniques.

Really any thought that pops into our conscious mind purposely or by accident is made possible to be read through Flip techniques. The more you practice mental telepathy, the more readable or transparent your thoughts will become especially to somebody close to you. **If you practice Flip on a daily basis and you exercise**

deception a lot, you are going to get caught at this deception. I think ridding the world of deception is one of the main purposes of telepathy. But alas we are only human and certain tolerances and adjustments will have to be made for the present by allowing and ignoring occasional bad thoughts by family and close acquaintances.

Most thoughts perceived leaking from a person's conscious through telepathy should be taken lightly. Bad thoughts of killing, rape, incest, etc., are normal daily thought occurrences. Currently in this world of gruesome serial killer books and movies this type of thinking seems to be the norm a lot. How some of these bestselling authors allow themselves to think this stuff is amazing. The author's fabrication of these stories must serve some purpose or they would not be so popular in the sales of these books and movies. **The point here is not to allow your mind to dwell on bad thoughts, unless of course you are viewing a 100 minute murder movie or reading a 400 page serial killer book novel; or of course writing one of these**. I don't know what people would think of me if I wrote serial killer books while at the same time being a master at telepathy and my mind's conscious thoughts were transparent. People would think I'm way out of my mind by them reading these thoughts if I wrote murder novel stuff.

I am just trying to illustrate that healthy minds entertain all kinds of bad thoughts on a normal daily basis and people around you will on occasion pick up on them through telepathy transparency of the conscious. Here we now begin to analyze the privacy of our thoughts. Casual observation of your thoughts and sometimes judgment of these thoughts will be passed from people around you and this will begin to happen more and more as you progress in Flip. **However when a person decides to continue to concentrate on your thoughts for more than 3 seconds without permission then this focus in my opinion constitutes an invasion of your privacy.** I think most of us would agree that this is a form of harassment. The same rules should also apply for transmitting thoughts into someone else's mind without permission and some type of politeness should be exercised with respect to other people's conscious space.

Many people read my thoughts even though I do not intend them to; this I call ***transparency***. I have been practicing Flip for more than 10 years now and this has facilitated the reading of my thoughts by other people without my conscious intentional push out of Flip. This reading of my mind does not pose much of a problem or embarrass me. Unless you are planning on lying to a lot of people or killing someone I do not think exposed conscious thoughts will ever pose much of an inconvenience for a normal person. It takes approximately 2 or 3 months to overcome this embarrassment of your transparent conscious thought through telepathy; and then you pay no attention to your conscious transparency reception by others.

It is human nature to be mean and aggressive in some form and this will naturally show up in some forms of Flip. I can only hope that the majority of people will exercise Ethics in association with mental telepathy. I truly think that the mental telepathy will help mankind to expand worldwide communication and therefore it must have ethical rules as it flows through our minds.

A lot of people push many of my own discarded thoughts back into my conscious with *summation Flip* that requires a little concentration on my part to repel. This pushing of discarded thoughts back into your conscious focus from the pre-conscious zone is unethical and I discuss this in detail in the chapter "Telepathic Examination of Other's Thought".

<u>I also want to say that a person should not try to interpret mental telepathy from television or the movies due to lack of synchronization in correct live time</u>. Trying to interpret Flip from these mediums will only confuse your mind. This is why I hope the movies and television will exercise restraint at the present time in the development of telepathy and remain free of Flip.

“If thoughts could kill”

Authors Capabilities

I the author have a gift to be a little more proficient at Flip then other people yet in time I hope others will be just as good as myself or better; for it would make me and my book lousy instructors if there were no replacements for me. Moving further into the future just about everybody will probably be experts at mental telepathy. I helped open the door to these new dimensions of thought transference and moving into the future the gains in resources will definitely be enormous.

I gave this Flip a life, but it now has a life and a course all its own and will soon be independent and free from my control. For this reason I try to write responsible rules for the things I have created. Keep in mind that **I create these theories of these new realities of the internal mind**; I then practice these new reality theories with many people to see if they agree and if they do agree with my thinking I write the truth about this new reality concept after its validation. (see Psychic Logic Blocks Chapter).

Many times I think about what should be in a logical sense, write it in my personal notes as wild theory and then over time I bring it forward into the public book as hard theory. You all can imagine what wild things I write for the good of mankind at 3 in the morning, some of which is mostly wild imagination that I keep in my personal notes. Some of my imaginative notes turn out to be total garbage to be thrown away and other stuff is hardened over time and brought forward into this book as future fact.

The Author (that's me) is able to put words under people's feet that seem to start under their feet and then progress the thought up through their legs and body and then into their mind. As a person moves with motion I am able to Flip words to the beat of the body motion such as head bounce. I have put words under people's feet from as far away as two miles from atop a tower in Las Vegas with the aid of a telescope.

I am able to touch people with telepathic image projection out to 5 kilometers or more. I able to control any sound I am hearing and interject with telepathy my own thoughts if desired and also I am able to destroy all sound Flip from other people within my hearing range. I am positive that if I could see the space shuttle as a reflective satellite at night, I could Flip images into the shuttle from any position on earth.

If you are anything like me, you believe nothing you hear and 1/2 of what you see. So how am I the author going to convince you about Flip? To begin with; Mankind is over 3.5 million years old and this is the first time foot talking and sound Flip has ever been done. Everyone does foot talking perfectly the first time they attempt it and sound Flip is just as easy to perform. Foot talking and sound Flip are very easy to perform and they are true forms of mental telepathy transmission. Mankind has now entered the new internal mind's dimensions of telepathy and so have you my friend.

I cannot regularly read a person's mind but many people are able to read almost all of my thoughts. I am slowly progressing towards reading other peoples mind but progress is slow for me in this area. Keep in mind that although I had a gift for telepathy I did not really start to develop it until I was 42 years old (1996). I cannot predict the future. Although I am capable of a lot of telepathy I keep thinking I'll wake up tomorrow and my capabilities for Flip will be gone. This does not matter to me and I do not think it should matter to the rest of the world either. Foot talking and sound Flip will hold mankind's grip on mental telepathy along with the children growing up including telepathy in their reality from the start of their life. Naturally I practice foot talking, sound Flip, motion, strobe, emotions, pure, and image mental telepathy. It is possible for me (the author) to take over the roar of a crowd of say 100,000 people in a football stadium and interject my thoughts with sound telepathy into the stadium crowd's noise. I am able to give the illusion that the ground is shaking slightly like a minor earth tremor.

When I join in with other people in image group summation I am able to receive their images transferred from them into my conscious mind during this agreed telepathy summation image projection group. I would like to point out that I need to have total trust with the people in the agreed mind transference summation group to be able to read image transmissions from them. Trust is needed for the lowering of all protective shielding of the conscious mind for reception of Flip images. If my conscious is the least bit afraid the image summation reception from other people in the group is not possible for me. Without this group trust or with the introduction of violence into the summation ring my mind will shut down to all telepathy reception as a protective device and I am quite sure other people in the group will also shut down telepathic reception.

Pure Flip should be able to go around the world with a trained family member or close friend. The receiver has to be trained for this long distance mental telepathy but many people do it well. Pure Flip is capable of going through solid objects; I have Flipped from 10 meters underwater hundreds of times to a distance of 1000 meters clearly. I can sound Flip the jet engines of jet fighter planes flying overhead at an air show, race car motors at the track, and all other motors along with other types of sound to a distance of 10 kilometers depending on the loudness of the sound. Fighter jets performing at an air show can be easily Flipped out to this 10 kilometer distance because the jet motors are so loud when flying close to the ground for the air show.

Mental Telepathy really started for me in 1996 while driving semi-truck and using the diesel engine exhaust brake to sound Flip with. Two years later I started foot talking in 1998. About a year and half after foot talking began we all started doing image Flips. When I was 14 years old a friend of mine would always say my words ahead of me. I like everyone else thought that this was a little weird and that possibly my friend could read minds a bit. I did not realize at 14 years old I had a gift for transmitting mental telepathy. It is also possible that my friend Don had a little telepathic ability and gave me a clue to this telepathy stuff.

Telekinesis and Anti -Telekinesis

Telekinesis is the setting of mass into motion with mental telepathy. I cannot set things into motion with telepathy; rather **it seems that I may be able to slow things already in motion a bit with telepathy. I am also positively able to deflect things already in motion with no mass such as radio waves using telepathy concentration.**

It might also be possible to deflect the Aurora Borealis with mental telepathy, as they are electromagnetic and contain very little mass. Curing cancer may be possible in the future by anti-telekinesis, by reducing the metabolism of the cancer cell thereby alerting antibodies to this particular cell because it is out of harmony with its surroundings. Cancer is also not a logical thing inside the internal body and should be attacked and cleansed.

Violent Telepathic Attacks

Violent telepathic thoughts are some of the most powerful occurring thoughts entering the conscious mind and they scare the mind causing it to shut itself off quickly as a defense against damage thereby stopping all higher functions of thinking. **On rare occasions violent attacks of mental telepathy will shock your mind and put it out of commission for a few hours by causing strong anxiety**. The mind is very strong but on some days the strongest may become victim at times to the shock of violent intrusion inside their mind by telepathy.

Telepathy has a way of getting inside your mind with thoughts and images and if violent may at times shock you. This shock effect can occur from a one on one attack or from a group of people summating against you.

These violent telepathy attacks are perceived inside your mind and scare the brain a lot more when attacking from the inside out. **<u>It is a shock to your mind that someone else is capable of walking around inside your personal brain doing harm</u>.** A close analogy would be people inside your mind with jack hammers of destruction, it freaks the mind out and it shuts down in a few seconds leaving an aftershock of anxiety.

This violent telepathic attack may last only for 3 to 5 seconds as the brain will protect itself right away from all attacks but the shock effect has taken place and done variable amounts of damage in the form of anxiety. The anxiety from some violent telepathic attacks will not be able to be stopped, as we are all human and sometimes lose mental control. However; as you learn the facts about violent telepathic attacks and that these ill effects will disappear in a short time anxiety will lessen. Do not let these violent attacks lead you into a paranoid condition that results in a loss of reality awareness. Telepathy and violent telepathic attacks are currently real and if I wanted I could even demonstrate a violent attack against someone.

Hang in there when these violent attacks of telepathy occur and try to avoid these mean people if possible.

I get startled from time to time by violent telepathic attacks but on one occasion over the 10 year period that I have practiced MT **someone got a good hard violent luck shot inside my mind.** I guess my brain was a little wore down from a lot of worry in my life during a week of real hard times and in my weakened condition my mind got too much of a shock. It had a shock effect to my mind occurring just a few hours before bedtime and in the morning there were no ill effects as I simply took a shower and went straight to bed for relief. Looking back at this incident it appears that since this was the first time this event ever happened to me I think I over reacted causing myself more problems than normal. This particular telepathic attack on me should have been down played but as you can see there were many variables involved here due to my weakened condition of stress and also it was my first experience with internal telepathic attacks.

Rarely do these telepathic attacks do more than startle your mind but you have to be aware that it is possible to shock the mind and cause anxiety for a few hours on rare occasions. I would also like to remind you to totally ignore the Flip attack if possible avoiding giving any validation to these evil people, which would make them stronger at these attacks in the future.

Gas Lighting is another form of a mental attack on a person's psyche. Normally another bad person says vocally bad words under their breath towards you when your back is turned. If you ask them if they said anything bad they will deny these bad words you heard when your back was turned. If the perpetrator gets good enough at these gas light bad words they will on occasion say them to your face and you may not know 100% of the time if these bad word cut downs were truly said by this particular bad person. Normal conversation loses 30% of words said, so gas lighting can be confusing as to the verification of this terrible trick.

The purpose of these gas light bad words behind your back or by introducing them into conversation in a sly way is to lower your self-esteem and also to undermine your sense of reality causing insanity. If these vocal gas lights are said by a close family member or another loved one who is very close then psychological damage will occur the very first time gas light words are used against you. Your human mind cannot accept the fact that a love one would try to hurt you so your mind gets extremely confused because it refuses to believe a loved one is really trying to hurt you with gas light words.

In a matter of a few minutes after gas lighting words by another loved one will result in permanent damage for the rest of your life with this gas lighting. This is hard to believe but rarely does a family member or person you love do this gas lighting to another loved one. If gas lighting occurs you cannot overcome it if it is a loved one doing it, or I should say a former loved one, because you will no longer be able to be near this particular person for the rest of your life, gas lighting by family causes paranoia in a few minutes that will continue for life with this former loved one.

If the bad person gas lighting you is not a family member or loved one this gas lighting will take some time to really make you sick, 2-3 weeks or maybe 2 months depending on the frequency of the attacks. The human mind knows that people who are not close to you may try to hurt you in a normal dog eat dog world fashion. The human mind is prepared to defend against these daily gas light attacks from strangers or fellow employees. If these attacks are allowed to be continued for weeks, then the perpetrator will at the least lower your self-esteem, cause stress, and anxiety. If gas lighting continues for 2 months or more the start of insanity by undermining your sense of reality will result from the perpetrator by denying he or she is gas lighting you. The trick here that makes the gas lighting effective is the denial by the evil person that they are doing it so your mind thinks that it may be hearing things.

The reason I describe gas lighting here is because this terrible verbal mental attack may also be carried out with foot talking, sound Flip, pure, or image telepathy and a person must be aware and prepared to ignore these attacks and move away from these people in the near future. Note: Gas Lighting is the name of an old movie starring Ingrid Bergman whose husband gas lighted her in the movie trying to drive her insane.

Another telepathic attack is done in the deep woods if one of the two or more people involved has some telepathic skills. A person may talk at a person for 2 kilometers or more in a normal voice volume and it will be heard but no sight of the person talking will be observed. This trick could undermine your sense of reality during a weekend of camping in the deep woods if camping alone. Three tricks are needed for this to work: 1 Voice aiming towards a particular victim. 2 - Telepathic skills by one. 3 - Hidden sender or senders. If aware of this trick and you have two or more people your friend would validate you and the joke would be on them. If alone and unaware in the deep woods this could be a problem. Remember that telepathy amplifies all senses and make adjustments in your mind for control.

One more great trick to undermine a person's reality that I have encountered in my travels is a crazy person talking at you from the middle of a cornfield at 2 or 3 in the morning; and of course all mental evil games do not need mental telepathy but telepathy is available for all evil.

Protecting Oneself from Telepathic Attacks

Protecting oneself from telepathic attacks will require a strong focused conscious in the future while in the public arena. Depending how well a person develops his or her skills at mind transference will determine his level of need for defenses against violent telepathic attacks. If a person such as myself goes out in public and I am known as a skilled telepathist then I will be tested by simple curiosity and jousted by some people as a test for their psychic powers; the "gunslinger scenario".

If totally relaxed while in public going into the future you will be open for attacks of psychic thoughts originating from outside your mind that may be inserted in your conscious that will startle, or the very least interrupt your train of thought with hate or simple debris. **The mind has strong and weak days according to stress and randomly may catch hurting thoughts more on some days than others.** Some type of repelling force field will be needed in public to repel telepathy.

So with mental telepathy increasing so will the need for a relaxed concentration barrier against unwanted telepathy in public. I say relaxed because it will be something like driving a car being in a state of concentration but being relaxed at the same time. When first learning a task maximum concentration is needed and then relaxed concentration takes over as the task becomes more facilitated making the task easier to perform. This protective barrier or conscious push away of these unwanted thoughts will be the same for all forms of telepathy.

When around family it is possible that they will together form a secure repelling force to intrusive thoughts when together in public and more so in the home. When with family it would be nice to lower one's conscious shields, especially in the home environment, conscious shielding a necessity that is needed in public for protection against unwanted mental telepathy. As mentioned before a family may learn to push out feelings of love with emotion Flip creating a loving ambiance and this pushing out of love in the home may also institute a passive protection in the home from outside bad thoughts and other forms of intrusive uninvited telepathy.

There is going to be revenge seeking people along with just plain bullies who are going to put together some type of synchronized attack at a calculated moment against individuals. **You will have to learn to lessen the startlement of the attack by rationalizing the interference as heavy traffic such as the rush hour commute in the big city.**

Cars and large trucks are constantly zooming dangerously close to your head in rush hour traffic but are deflected away by your conscious thoughts resulting in staying safely in your lane on the highway while driving. In time telepathic attacks will be able to be deflected to another area of the mind such as deflecting the image down and away from your imagined area of conscious thinking and into the dark area of the pre-cognitive zone.

REMEMBER, NO MIND CAN REFUSE ONE OF MY IMAGES OR THOUGHTS SO BE AWARE AND BEGIN TO PROTECT YOURSELF NOW!

Pre-Conscious Subliminal Images
(Low Energy Thoughts)

Subliminal thought by this book's definition means thoughts lacking psychic energy for breaking the threshold barrier of the conscious threshold viewing window and snapping into the conscious for recognition. This conscious threshold viewing window creates a stopping or repelling barrier for low energy thoughts keeping them from entering or disturbing the conscious. Thoughts of high energy automatically snap into the conscious without selection.

Many forming thoughts appear to be super quick flickers in the obscure area of the pre-conscious holding no light, seen only as dark images on a dark background. Subliminal in nature with hardly any form at all, yet almost recognized as a formed thought even though lacking completeness and detail. When these images have no conscious dwell or focus on them, they are perceived as dark gray images on gray-black background or light black images on gray-black background. The contrast here is practically non-existent yet these images appear and they are scanned quickly as they pass the ***conscious threshold viewing window***.

If a subliminal thought in this dark stage is interesting to the conscious attention it will then be focused on giving it illumination and detail according to the degree of conscious concentration put on this pre-conscious concept and possible now brought forward into the conscious gallery for full examination through the conscious threshold viewing window.

If the subliminal thought is low in energy or is uninteresting to the conscious mind it will be ignored causing this uninteresting thought to now be deflected away from the conscious threshold viewing window and this particular thought now heads for deep space.

These dark images are rough sketches for the mind as the conscious gallery does not want to take the time to illuminate and detail every thought zooming by in the background in the pre-conscious. If this constant flow of pre-cognitive thoughts were allowed to enter the conscious it would be packed full of unwanted thoughts and nothing would be accomplished due to lack of concentration on pertinent thought, which is conscious selected by the will of the conscious mind from physical world instructions, short term memory or long term memory for construction of a concept.

I would like to point out here that I think the darkness or void that the pre-cognitive thoughts are hiding in is needed for containment of these thoughts here in the pre-conscious to prevent them from leaking into the conscious total awareness and breaking concentration. Although brightly colored and detailed images in the brain are important, so is the total darkness that is the protective dam of the pre-conscious for keeping trash from coming into the conscious focus. Ideas in this pre-conscious area are sometimes referred to as tip of the tongue concepts that are almost recognized in the conscious but not quite totally seen yet or remembered due to incompleteness, low detail, or no matching which results in low psychic energy that fails to break threshold level.

When a person's conscious mind becomes interested in a subliminal image in the pre-conscious zone of another person's mind other than the originator it will illuminate and detail the image through **telepathic summation focus.** This focus of another person's mind upon the originator's pre-cognitive thought gives this pre-conscious thought enough psychic energy to now be recognized by the conscious breaking threshold into the conscious of the originator, as well as the conscious of the other person viewing and energizing it. This is psychic summation energy that provides adequate psychic energy to a pre-conscious thought to break threshold into both the consciouses now. **This meaning another person can power up your own weak pre-conscious thoughts or recently discarded conscious thoughts for you by summating them with observation telepathy or dwell**. In addition focus from another person also allows this now psychic energized pre-conscious thought to now snap into the consciouses of all people in close proximity (100 meters) through summation, that automatically snaps the thought into the universal mind.

All the thoughts in the pre-conscious that are close to the conscious threshold viewing window contain high psychic energy and thus an affinity for closeness to this window but do not possess enough recognition energy to break through the conscious threshold window by themselves.

Thoughts hovering closest to this conscious threshold viewing window will most likely be the high psychic energy thoughts that other people view with telepathy. High psychic energy thoughts of the pre-conscious zone include the most recently discarded thoughts from the conscious that are normally about 2 to 3 minutes in past history, which contain high residual psychic energy and in addition some high energy pre-conscious thoughts that lack completeness.

Telepathic Examination of Others Thoughts Transparency and Summation

It is a sure fire truth to say that a lot of people are going to be practicing mental telepathy in the near future. This will facilitate a lot more examination of other people's thoughts through the human mind's thought transparency as a result of practicing telepathy for any length of time; say 2 years or more. The longer a person exercises mind transference the greater this transparency of conscious, transparency of short term memory and also the transparency of pre-conscious thoughts will be to the public. The owner of these transparent conscious thoughts will remain hidden unless around friends, family, or a small group where familiarity and deduction will fix his or her identity. In addition simple constant close proximity to the same individuals will eventually lead to the discovery of the originator of a telepathic thought. It is normal progression for an expert of mental telepathy to not have to send thoughts out of conscious but only think normally and others will detect his or her conscious thoughts very easily; and sometimes high energy short term memory and pre-conscious thoughts as well.

Amateurs practicing telepathy will also leak thoughts in to an agreed physical world synchronized point unintentional at times and all people in 100 meter proximity will perceive the amateurs thoughts somewhat like the masters transparency.

Note: The long term memory's thoughts are normally not available for telepathic examination or do they normally exhibit transparency.

The long term memory is protected more than the short term memory, pre-conscious or conscious from outside inspection from others. The long term memory will however automatically add what it knows to a telepathy transmission and does not always need to be retrieved by conscious selection when summation telepathy is occurring but the long term memory does not exhibit transparency.

Normally for conscious transparency to be possible one of the participants in this summation must be required to be proficient at telepathy but this is not always the rule. Some close friends or family members might not need to be proficient at telepathy in order to pick up on leaking transparent thought but rather use simple casual ***mental telepathy drift***.

An important factor here for powering up others thoughts with telepathy summation is being in close proximity or within sight distance of an individual, this makes it a lot easier to key in on his or her thoughts. Again an exception to the general rule is a close family member or friend who may be in another country and these Flip summations will happen but generally speaking this takes place within 100 meters.

Conscious thoughts possess the most psychic energy and thus will be the easiest to view through telepathy transparency. Some of the thoughts that were previously in the conscious focus have been cleared away into the pre-conscious zone or have been recognized as bad thoughts and repelled back into the pre-conscious zone of the originator.

These discarded or repelled conscious thoughts (now presently in the pre-conscious area) still possess high residual psychic energy but are steadily moving away from the conscious threshold window reducing awareness as time progresses (a type of Doppler Effect). These discarded conscious thoughts are now high-energy pre-conscious thoughts. The pre-conscious also has other high energy thoughts some incomplete that have never made the conscious view due to lacking the necessary psychic energy to break the threshold barrier.

Most previous conscious thoughts are filed into the short term memory automatically, and some are deemed pertinent to also be filed into the long term memory. The newly encoded short term memory thought presently sits first on top of the pile of thoughts in the short term memory diminishing in power with added time and moving down the ladder of power in this stored pile of thoughts. As these thoughts move down the pile in the short term memory they decrease in energy and eventually leave the short term memory through dreaming through the pre-conscious. Some of the more recently filed short term memory thoughts possess high psychic energy and will leak back into the pre-conscious zone at times and may be drawn back towards the conscious threshold viewing window.

All these discarded and incomplete thoughts now lie in the pre-conscious zone and possess high energy but are lacking sufficient energy to break the conscious threshold barrier into the conscious. These high energy pre-conscious thoughts are available to be powered up by other people examining your pre-conscious zone with telepathy. Telepathic focus from another person adds more psychic energy to a particular pre-conscious thought and now this pre-conscious thought will break the conscious threshold barrier of the originator as the other person supplies added psychic energy, this whole process is referred to as ***summation telepathy.***

Summation Psychic Energy will bring these pre-cognitive thoughts forward into conscious view (some of these thoughts will be appearing in the originator's conscious for a second time) through the focus of another person's telepathy. **In addition the summation telepathy of others may help assemble missing pieces extracted from all their memories to the originators pre-cognitive concept.** This summation Flip of others allows the concept to be completed and then this will now enable all consciouses in close proximity to recognize and pull forward the thought for viewing into their conscious galleries; usually this is done automatically by all the consciouses in the immediate vicinity about 100 meter radius.

Normally the highest energy thoughts will break the threshold barrier and be drawn automatically and immediately into the conscious. Thoughts with high energy but not enough energy to break the conscious threshold barrier will stay in the middle ground or pre-conscious. As mentioned before these high energy pre-conscious zone thoughts will have a great affinity for the ***conscious threshold viewing window*** hanging close by this window. People that are able to view and summate your pre-conscious thoughts will generally be detecting these particular high energy thoughts hovering near the conscious threshold viewing window. These pre-conscious thoughts are the easiest to notice but still lack enough energy to break into the conscious for total clear focus.

Discarded conscious concepts may be re-energized again breaking threshold energy into the conscious focus for the second time without the approval or conscious selection of the originator of the thought through summation examination of others. Actually this is an insertion of a type of sickness called compulsive thinking, definitely not totally good. A lot of telepathy summated thoughts may prove to be a total distraction causing dysfunction of higher thought processes in the conscious mind of the originator by these unselected pre-conscious summated thoughts. Over time this potpourri of Flip summated pre-conscious thoughts must be learned to be ignored and repelled away from your conscious focus back into the pre-conscious.

This whole thought process of uninvited intrusion into an individual's mind begins when another **person or persons begins to focus and linger on your personal thoughts without permission, which will be considered unethical in most instances.** A simple scanning of another person's thoughts is quite normal but to dwell on another person's thoughts for more than 3 seconds without permission is usually going to be wrong. **I say usually wrong because if there is something too far out of line from normal thinking then this will definitely draw attention and warrant examination by others.**

A criminal conscious mind dwelling for long periods of time on unlawful subjects will pick up constant judgment from the world conscience because this fellow is way out of the furrow and may do harm to the people of society. This person with abnormal thoughts will highlight him or herself in public, and may also have violent thoughts that are the most powerful telepathic thoughts and he or she will most definitely draw close scrutinization to their thinking by others.

Anti-social thoughts may require intrusive examination by others that will then power up these bad thoughts with mental telepathy summation for the good of the individual or society such as a warning to prevent injury or to prevent a crime.

People will be examining the minds of others with telepathy for anything interesting in the conscious or the pre-cognitive junkyard, telepathy focus on pre-cognit*ive* thoughts will power up these thoughts up and snap them into the conscious now. Only a short dwell time of focus on these pre-cognitive thoughts will provide enough psychic energy to break threshold and then shoot them forward into the conscious creating interference. Probably not all these summated thoughts by others will be bad thoughts but most of these powered up thoughts will be not wanted by the conscious of a private person.

As long as there is not too much dwell time applied to these pre-conscious thoughts they will be able to be repelled back into the pre-cognitive zone from conscious focus without too much problem. **Anymore than say three seconds dwell time and these pre-conscious thoughts will really pick up power and break the conscious threshold energy barrier and be viewed in the conscious galleries of both people with clarity and be hard to repel away now.**

This dwell focus of more than three seconds on another's thoughts, unless a warning to prevent injury or examining violent thoughts will be looked upon as unethical harassment.

Again, unless a warning to avoid injury to a person or society you should merely glance at another person's internal thoughts and then look away, think of something else quickly, or possible say to yourself in an internal voice pardon me, or stop. Of course a lot of people's internal thoughts are going to be quick scanned for less than 3 seconds and this will occur throughout the day and will not pose a problem.

If you do intrude into another person's mind and create a bad sequence of thoughts it would be proper and helpful for you to help repel these thoughts by simply not allowing them to enter your conscious mind because both you and the originator of thought must work together to repel this particular thought back to the pre-conscious.

How about a retarded person dwelling on peoples' thoughts who does not know any better? Mental telepathy is a great help for the mentally handicapped and so a lot of these people will be taught telepathy to aid their minds with communication. These mentally retarded people may be a little uncontrollable and crowd their teacher's mind or yours for that matter with Flip.

It is plain to see that a lot of people will not follow harassment rules and most of the time you will not know what individual is powering up your trash thoughts; generally they will be in a 100 meter radius of you. The people of this new telepathic world will have to put up a force field of resistance to these bad people powering up our trash thoughts or we all will get our thoughts scrambled and lose our train of thought in the conscious zone.

Society will automatically begin to enforce the practice of *Ethical Manners* concerning the intrusion and focusing on other people's thoughts without permission. This will be carried out through the attention of the ***world conscience*** and its moral weight brought to bear chastising individuals for wrong choices and incorrect thinking by the world society as a whole. Of course scanning another person's mind for more than 3 seconds is wrong and should be noticed by other people around you. A sick criminal (for example a child molester) must not be allowed to think thoughts about raping children for more than 3 seconds. Anymore than 3 seconds dwell time on this particular criminal act will in essence be a real conscious plan being fabricated to accomplish this scenario in the future.

With the addition of telepathy the conscious at times in the future may be compared to what some psychologists refer to as the cocktail party analogy. When at a cocktail party everybody is talking at once yet two people usually do not have too much of problem communicating to one another over the room full of other conversations and noise of the party. The conscious for brief times is going to probably take on this interference scenario if only for short bursts from other's telepathy before coming under control and being ignored.

Your powered up internal thoughts from summation telepathy of others should be with practice be able to be ignored unless they continued to be dwelled upon; or given a vocalized repetition of the thought that would then etch the thought in stone.

Some people become super adept at reading others people's thoughts through mental telepathy and they sometimes repeat right away with vocal repetition what your next conscious thought is going to be. A few people are capable of doing this voice repeating of your approaching conscious thought before you think it making the thought seem as if it was theirs and not yours. It is extremely impressive how quick some people can say your next conscious thought before you think it but very, very, annoying and impolite.

Ownership and Moral Responsibility of Thought

Thoughts with super high energy automatically move into the conscious and are held with focus in the conscious gallery for examination. When a thought is cleared from the conscious the thought moves away from the conscious for encoding into the memories or is thrown into pre-conscious universe as unwanted debris or possible both sequences occur at the same time. Concepts when first discarded from the conscious still possess a lot of residual recognition energy but currently not enough to break the energy threshold barrier and re-enter the conscious.

All previous conscious thoughts are filed into the short term memory automatically. **This presently encoded short term memory thought now sits on top of the pile of thoughts in the short term memory diminishing in power with time, moving down the pile of thoughts and eventually leaving the short term memory through dreaming after 72 hours.**

Randomly these short term memory thoughts may leak back into the pre-conscious zone. The primitive mind also coughs forward its pre-cognitive thoughts of wants and needs of hunger, shelter, sex, and violence that constantly seem to be floating near the conscious threshold viewing window but lacking enough energy to break into the conscious awareness. These primitive mind thoughts have high power but most of the time not enough to break into the conscious and in addition a lot of primitive mind thoughts have to be repressed due to being socially unacceptable. These thoughts are constantly trying to enter the conscious as all primitive thoughts are needed for survival of the human animal to some degree.

The other non-important thoughts cleared from the conscious will simply be thrown into the pre-conscious zone as trash and possess less power than a short term memory thought diminishing in power a lot more rapidly. **The longer a thought was dwelled on in the conscious the more residual power it will contain in the pre-conscious zone and short term memory of originator to spring forward again**

with the help of telepathic examination from other people supplying psychic energy. These pre-conscious zone thoughts lose power rapidly; and again the short term memory thoughts gradually lose power and are totally gone in three days (72 hours) through dreaming.

The long term memory is protected more than the short term memory, pre-conscious or conscious from outside inspection from others. The long term memory will however automatically add what it knows to a telepathy transmission and does not always need to be retrieved by conscious selection when summation telepathy is occurring but the long term memory does not exhibit transparency of thoughts it contains to others.

Ownership of Thought

For all practical purposes your thought belongs to you only when it is in your conscious mind being viewed, or for a time of approximately 3 minutes in the pre-conscious zone after being discarded from the conscious and an equal simultaneous time of 3 minutes on the top of the short term memory, and finally it is your thought when in the long term memory that must be retrieved by the *conscious will* of the originator.

Previously viewed conscious thoughts that are discarded into the pre-conscious are constantly moving away from the conscious threshold viewing window growing more distant in the pre-conscious and are your personal thoughts in the universe only when relatively close to your conscious threshold viewing window in the form of time. The longer the amount time the thought travels from your conscious threshold window, the less the thought belongs to you unless filed into the long term memory, and then only your thought becoming available by your personal conscious selection of this particular thought.

The conscious threshold viewing window has an affinity for high-energy thoughts from the pre-conscious or short term memory that enables these high energy thoughts to remain for a longer period of time close to this window, and then moving away slower than a low energy thought would do. A pre-conscious thought with high energy will hover close to the conscious threshold viewing window and it is this thought that has the best chance of snapping back for a 2nd time into the conscious of the originator with the telepathy focus of another or summation.

Extra psychic energy from telepathic summation of another person helps to energize your pre-conscious or short term memory thought with psychic energy thereby enabling both consciouses to now recognize this thought. A thought can originate from anywhere in the universe and go anywhere in the universe with the introduction of mental telepathy practices.

A person is aware of his own created thought while viewing it in the conscious gallery and for approximately 3 minutes after disposal into the short term memory or pre-conscious zone growing fainter in perception with the increase of time. Again a thought may be filed into the long term memory where others cannot view it through transparency of mind yet it may be added to another concept not originating in the long term memory through summation telepathy automatically or may be retrieved by the conscious selection of the originator but not by casual observation of another through telepathy.

Moral Responsibility of Thought

Moral responsibility for a thought is only yours while being viewed in your conscious gallery. If another person pushes one of your own discarded conscious thoughts that now lies in your pre-conscious zone back into your conscious view with their telepathy focus then you will not be responsible for another person's conscious selection of your discarded conscious thoughts. Moral responsibility for this pre-conscious psychic re-energized thought will now be the fault of the "other person" who was dwelling on your discarded conscious thought for too long of a time, approximately 3 seconds, which is an unethical action.

Responsibility must be taken for downloading too much violence into the short term memory, as this will begin to leak out if in abundance and show up in the single mind of the universe by the scanning and energizing of the pre-conscious zone, which will contain these bad thoughts. I am at a loss to state the amount of violence the short term memory should be allowed to take in over its 72-hour time period but caution must be exercised nonetheless. If some violence is normal for the functioning of the human life, then it must be controlled and managed.

New Realities and Skepticism in Telepathy

A true psychic has to also be a skeptic to compensate for the truly magnificent imagination that he or she possesses. A psychic has to be a non-believing skeptic to a point; as a way to counterbalance the wild ideas that will naturally crop up in a creative mind that is doing the impossible by changing present day realities. Fact is, you already are doing the impossible so why not keep going and levitate or do something even more futuristic?

If the human mind jumps too far ahead in new realities then it is balancing its shaky new realities on flimsy ground and will lose all new attained ground falling back to the solid basic logic foundation blocks again. This failure of telepathy advancement will temporarily destroy confidence for building forward again.

The psychic wishes a lot were true in order to help mankind, but this ESP stuff has to end somewhere, if not only for the present time.

A man loves to run down the road of imagination a good long way before encountering the turning around point checking back with his validated realities once again. The human mind stops on its own when it becomes a little scared or disoriented in its travel through the new dimensions of reality inside the internal mind. The human mind thirsts heavily for this advanced communication of mental telepathy with its resources from other dimensions and speeds toward its goals of perfect communication searching for new data on its own accord and time, which is 24 hours a day without conscious permission throughout the universe.

The mind will constantly push the envelope of new realities but always remain in clear view of the solid reality it has constructed behind its course. **As the mind travels through these new dimensions it is constantly checking back with its factual data to keep oriented and sane.** In this way the mind is able to build new realities always strengthening its foundations of new realities before it goes forward in time or travel again. The human mind will always perform this way taking brief rest stops here and there for a few months or years before looking further ahead in new realities in order to form a solid base camp before moving forward again towards the infinity of perfection.

The automatic intelligence of a person will know when they should not push forward anymore until we all form a solid foundation in these new areas, retreating if necessary to these strong foot holds when confidence wanes and anxiety strikes. For now we have to say no to things that will logically take place in the future like curing cancer with telepathy of the mind.

I know we will cure cancer and other diseases with telepathy this being a logical concept as the human mind knows no boundaries but logic yet at this time we say it is impossible for the present because we need to build towards this goal a step at a time.

Telepathy is fantastic and sometimes requires unimaginable faith, but somehow we must believe in its future. This book **FLIP** will build a solid foundation for mental telepathy to build on creating future new realities.

Universal Language

The Flip Universal Language is composed of images of real life scenarios forming communication that is shown as actual real life images that occur naturally in the external environment. Pictograph Flip image projection can be perceived throughout the universe with no problem forming the only true universal language in the entire universe as long as the individuals being communicated with are intelligent beings.

Cognitive symbols or words are not interchangeable with other languages. Although they are recognized as the correct symbol or word image totally, the concept associated with the image seen is not always understood as it is unfamiliar in its meaning by matching. A set of ordered cognitive symbols or words in one language is not universally recognizable or perceived as the intended matching concept in another language, yet Flip image language will be understood by all that see it in the universe.

Examples: Images of food projected with telepathy while being consumed would be something all living creatures would recognize such as a fruit or drink. Meat or hamburger Flip image projections shown to aliens could be misinterpreted as hostile leading to big trouble in the far universe and possible get a ray gun trained on you! A person will need to use fruits and vegetables as image projections for food to refrain from hostile images of killing living creatures to sustain oneself; funny but true. Any social or other normal daily occurring event should be able to be image Flipped and understood by any intelligent being in the universe.

Death

Flip does not use normal energy but psychic energy that is not to be defined but accepted as a given. Psychic energy has to be powerful and faster than the speed of light for time jumping back and forth the way it does. In theory telepathy travels to the farthest corner of the universe and back again instantly in internal mind to mind concepts. Since telepathy is some type of psychic energy but not physical energy it may be possible that after death even though the physical brain is dead, telepathic thoughts of this nature may continue to function with psychic energy.

In the dark of death telepathy thought may spring forward again trying for summation telepathy with other people to strike a light in this darkness and begin thinking in this other dimension, the dimension of death. With billions of people in the dead dimension, it seems as though some the individuals who practiced telepathy in life will be able to get illumination and communication going to some degree after death in this dead dimension. If true; is this eternity of thought really a curse of boredom forever or a godsend of heaven? Psychic energy may still be available for thought in this dead dimension.

A live person on earth capable of telepathic illumination may be able to enter into the dead zone for channeling with the dead.

If thinking continues after death then in **theory** a dead person's thoughts may return by telepathy to this world and be born again in another's mind or become a parasite in another live person's mind. We will have to be aware and watch for peculiar thoughts in the future that occur in each others' mind. If all this telepathic thought is possible after death then the world conscience will look for these types of thoughts and police the telepathic thought no matter where they are originating from in time or place in the universe.

Since evil is not logical it should be sought out and destroyed in the universe by summation telepathy and the world conscience.

Laws to Protect Psychics

Trying to irritate or give duress to a Psychic person is not a great reward for a person who has either trained their mind to help mankind or may have been born with these gifts of telepathic ability. Some Psychics will have to hide from society to protect their minds from irritation or damage. Not every Psychic will be able to take the constant increase in stimulation from all the people of this world. This hiding is not what the world should want for a valuable teacher of telepathy communication skills. Nobody will venture far into thought transference areas if the only rewards are torture and ostracization. Some people would prefer to enslave a gifted person and use them as a tool for communication or for destruction at their convenience.

To protect one's mind from attack and stay healthy with a "strong will" the Psychic and all the people in society (I hope to think some day in the future all people will be telepathic) will have to maintain a strong telepathic rebuttal in their mind to stave off evil attacks of telepathy.

These rebuttals will not be nice and we now begin to use bad telepathic words and image Flips that telepathy was supposed to help correct.

Unfortunately we are all currently living in an imperfect world that we are all working to correct and we must be tolerant as we begin to make these adjustments with Flip. We are beginning to form the **world conscience** but this will take some time allowing people for now to go unchecked at times. Some unethical defenses will be necessary to combat the terrible things or attacks that people will bring against a psychic or another person. A person may become strong in the practice of ignoring violent attacks but this takes years of practice and everybody will not be able to totally ignore these attacks of telepathy 100% of the time. So a person will at times have to fight back with nasty rebuttals or their mind will suffer and become sick.

Telepaths can be used in this fashion as a weapon for hurting other people's feelings as they are made angry and provoked into a sarcastic rebuttal that many others may hear. **Most of the time in this world it is easier and more fun to hurt peoples' feelings tearing them down; rather than to love them and build them up.** As psychic energy builds for communication a telepath must exercise moral restraint when it becomes necessary to vent a little stress. The sadistic choice may be easier and again more fun. So the time is now to institute laws to protect the psychic.

Love requires the strongest mind;

violence is the easy route to vent Psychic energy or stress.

Citizens Band Radio

Citizens band radio feedback squeal is a favorite tool of MAD mothers and some Neighborhood Watches. With a special digital radio tuner children can be crippled by a common citizens band radio or police radio. The nerves can be shorted out in the child's knees and the child will fall down twisting his knee destroying it for life. I know this is hard to believe but I have personally witnessed this weapon in use hundreds of times. This is a fact known to a lot of evildoer's that radios can be used as weapons and all people need to take note. These intense radio waves could facilitate pre-schooler's immature minds that might form deviant harmful neural pathways that facilitate lots of useless busy work for the young mind.

Blood flow may also be slowed down by the effect of the radio waves partially closing valves located in the small capillary blood vessels in the brain and artificial stroke may be induced. Not only does it close blood vessel valves but it also causes high blood pressure that may damage the small blood vessels in the retina of the eye. Nerve deafness may also occur from various different techniques of these sociopath radio tricks. In addition asthma in children may easily be induced with this radio feedback squeal as it stresses the child's lung muscles and breathing system.

Sometimes the radio waves are felt and other times they are not. The favorite trick of the sociopath is to turn this radio weapon on their victim at three o'clock in the morning while they sleep and when the person wakes up they have some type of physical damage or a simple migraine headache. Radio waves are suspected of being the number one cause of breast cancer in the United States and I also suspect birth defects to the unborn fetus by these strong radio waves.

Citizen band radios are being made into a deadly weapon and these radio wave attacks affect various people in different ways and this great "tool" must be licensed and policed. This radio wave feedback also breaks down the conscious barrier wall and the conscious mind becomes flooded with lots of useless trash from the pre-conscious zone. This gives the mind a compulsive thinking sickness and anguish for children especially with their eyes closed while trying to sleep.

I am a strong psychic that allows me to fall prey to these radios squealing as my nerves are sensitive and this radio squealing is beyond belief painful for me. At times this radio squealing makes my mind insane and I want to kill people, while at the same time a little girl in front of me stares at me in disbelief because she cannot feel the radio squeal. The curse of having telepathy, super sense perception due to the amplification at times to certain stimulus.

VOCABULARY

Agreed Physical World Synchronization Points - An agreed shared physical synchronization point may be sound, vibration or light; the agreement part here is the knowledge by two or more people that these physical facts exist and are agreed on by two or more people. Used as auxiliary helpers to synchronize a conscious thought into the universal mind.

Artificial Memory Sound - Sounds implanted by telepathy techniques into the long term memory of an individual and retrieved with telepathy for artificial sound replication from the long term memory.

Auxiliary Helper - a sound, light, touching, or vibration to help synchronize thoughts and give confidence for performing telepathy.

Channeling - communicating with the non-living in the dead dimension.

Cognitive - higher thinking processes. Knowing or perception to learn.

Cognitive Symbols - language, alphabets, words and images. Cognitive symbols provide placeholders in the mind; holding the thought in the conscious for clearer examination. Prevents concept from slipping away and allows for easy memory file and storage of the thought by categorizing.

Collective Conscience is a living memory that is just now being created with Flip that stores all logical and moral majority thoughts used for comparison to your own present conscious thinking. Operated and policed by the World Conscience. Collective Conscience exerts pain pressure through the amplifying of guilt and anxiety of wrong choices.

Collective Conscious - a group, tribe, country, or the total brains in the entire world sharing awareness of the same present thoughts through telepathy summation.

Concentration - time held in conscious for study.

Conscience - sense of what is right or wrong. Morals stored in long term memory.

Conscious - concepts viewed in this area of the mind are recognized and senses perceived, full image saturation here, attention focused on the totally exposed thought here. Will power and decision making. Thoughts retrieved from memories intentionally from this area of command. Awareness of Concepts.

Conscious Will - the power to make intentional decisions and chose one of many options that are favorable to the mind. Voluntary Conscious Selection.

Consciousness - a noun signifying awareness of the same thoughts.

Conscious Gallery - images projected inside the mind with conscious focus onto this internal mind's screen.

Conscious Threshold Barrier is a wall that keeps unwanted thoughts from entering into the conscious from the pre-conscious zone. When a thought possesses enough energy it is able to be recognized by the conscious's focus and now break through this barrier and snap into the conscious.

Conscious Threshold Viewing Window - an area slightly open to the pre-conscious for viewing pre-cognitive thoughts. Recently discarded conscious thoughts sometimes linger here for a short time. Thoughts with high energy automatically snap into the conscious focus through here sometimes with telepathy summated energy.

Conscious Transparency - with the increased practice of mental telepathy the conscious mind automatically begins to be viewed by all people in close proximity, normally within 100 meters. In addition the most recent parts of the short term memory and a few pre-conscious high energy thoughts are able to be viewed by this phenomenon.

Container - field of psychic energy that holds all thoughts.

Depth Perception - measured and compared images in a three-dimensional background.

Dimensional levels - space and time measurement. Areas of the internal human mind containing different characteristics and resources. Many times additional image construction resources in the multitude of levels with thoughts traveling the entire universe and back again instantaneously.

Directional Flip - the aiming of telepathy with sound or moving a foreign sound to a new location; possible moving a sound as to appear as if coming from another person's mouth.

Disinhibited - not caring what others think about your present behavior.

Doors - Telepathy Techniques unlock doors to a multitude of dimensions for using resources in that dimension.

Dream Suggestion - An awake conscious person talks to a sleeping person suggesting dream image construction while they sleep. Fantastic image constructions.

Dual Attachment is attaching a minor thought almost subliminal in nature simultaneously to a major totally clear and much stronger thought with mentally telepathy projection.

Dwell - the time spent examining a concept, the greater amount of this focus time, the more energy the thought possesses. Dwell is one of the things capable of providing the energy necessary to break the threshold barrier between the pre-conscious and conscious.

E.S.P. - Extra Sensory Perception. Perception or communication outside normal senses such as mental telepathy.

Ethical Policing - world conscience putting stress on a person's conscious to stay in the furrow of normalcy.

Facilitation - operations of the brain or body that are made easier to do over time by the lowering of resistance in a particular neural pathway due to numerous previous impulses (practicing).

Facilitated Pathway Branching - stimulating and building more neural pathways in the newborn's brain increasing intelligence and having alternate neural pathways for repairing possible future physical damage with the help of telepathy.

FLIP - is a nickname for mental telepathy.

F.L.I.P. - future link intelligent people.

Focus - concentrated viewing by the conscious mind. Time spent understanding concept by the conscious mind.

Forms - things created that are the perfect archetype for construction of concepts and comparison of correct moral thinking. In some schools of philosophy all the forms of all things present and future have already been created and are passed down when mankind needs them or is capable of understanding them.

Gallery - an area inside the conscious mind that contains viewing screens for viewing and assembling images.

Group Summation - individuals in co-operation for the same goal using telepathy techniques for constructing and enhancing shared construction of such goals.

Illumination - light or brightness for clearer observation.

Image Saturation - amount of detail, visible mass, or the coloring in the picture.

Imagination - the power of forming mental images of concepts not seen by the physical senses. Creations of the internal mind.

Logic Block - a concept based on internal mind's capabilities and logic for telepathy. Logic blocks must agree with other telepathy foundation blocks; building complex functions from many logic blocks for accomplishing mental tasks. Logic blocks do not have to obey physical law, only logic but must be proven. If faulty telepathic logic block is inserted in the foundation sequence then function failure will result and the concepts constructed will collapse and fall back to the primary known logic blocks. This falling back will result in confusion and lost time.

Mental Telepathy Drift - incomplete mental telepathy, yet partial reception is often realized. Mental telepathy lacking psychic energy synchronization.

Mind Meld - minds coming together forming one mind for communication and enrichment of concepts through more available resources.

Mind Transference - another name for telepathy or mind to mind exchange of ideas.

Moral Responsibility of Thought - rests with the person who is focusing on present thought and giving it energy no matter where viewed.

Neural Network - nervous system pathways hooked together forming larger system.

Neurotic - person who cannot filter out stimulus resulting in slight confusion and at times anxiety attacks that temporary incapacitate. Some people take filtering drugs such as valium for reduced stimulus and others simply live with this minor affliction. Many neurotics get better with age on their own without counseling or drugs but this normally takes years. If it took you 10 years to get sick as a neurotic it with generally take 10 years to get better on your own. With counseling time may be shortened but is extremely expensive due to time of cure.

Non-jugdemental Friend - a friend who will help a person and not hold their past misdeeds against them, which is necessary for helping a mentally ill person. A judgemental person will be detrimental to helping their mentally ill friend.

Occurrence - happening at a specific time.

Originator - is the person who first thinks or transmits this thought with telepathy.

Ownership of Thought - the person who originally created this particular thought.

Paranoid Schizophrenic - Out of touch with reality on a daily basis. Stress causes worsening of present condition. On occasion has auditory and visual hallucinations. Sometimes made better or close to normal with daily dose of medications or monthly injections.

Pathway - nervous system transfer branch or route for carrying thought.

Perception - awareness through senses of stimulus data. Ability to recognize and construct incoming data from sensory input including non-physical data of mental telepathy.

Physical Auxiliary Helpers - a sound, light, touching, or vibration to help synchronize thoughts and give confidence for performing telepathy. Used interchangeably with agreed physical synchronization points.

Physical Energy - bio-chemical reactions in the neural pathways and brain that manufacture energy for thinking processes and synchronization of psychic energy resulting in capturing thought.

Piggyback Senses - integrate one nervous system pathway onto another using bio-chemical energy for synchronizing a thought, which then helps contains and transport the thought along to the conscious.

Pre-Cognitive - a concept not quite recognized by the conscious yet. Sometimes fades in and out of conscious perception briefly returning to pre-conscious area if lacking energy. Some scientists refer to this as the tip of tongue concept where a thought is forming but is a little weak and lacks completeness. May be interchanged freely with the terms pre-conscious thought, subliminal thought, or sub-conscious.

Pre-Conscious - large area possibly containing the entire universe here. This area contains weak thoughts or bits and pieces of partial concepts. Vague imprints of images just out of reach of conscious awareness. Summation telepathy can occur here between two or more human minds completing partial thoughts or powering up weak thoughts through psychic dwell by other people's telepathic examination of the concept. Many thoughts here are in the dark, with no illumination or detail, fleeting by conscious threshold viewing window. A type of Disorganized Temporary Memory. Empties out the short term memory by dreaming over approximately 72 hours. Exchanged freely with the terms pre-cognitive area, subliminal zone, or sub-conscious.

Primitive Mind - the matching of conscious physical sensory input with chemical memory templates for basic attractions and repulsions of the primitive human mind.

Projection - a push out from the conscious mind of a concept or image into outside world.

Psychic Dwell is the telepathic focus of another person who focuses on one of your own thoughts that is made available for viewing by transparency of mind.

Psychic Energy - fields of energy that contain all thought and when synchronized more than once telepathy viewing and transmission is possible. Mental telepathy power for recognition and transmission of thoughts, which does not obey physical law. All thought is contained by psychic energy and it is this psychic energy that provides the ***vehicle*** for thought transmission. Chapter titled Psychic Energy page 12.

Psychic Energy Container - field of psychic energy that holds all thoughts of the universe. Human mind captures these packets of psychic energy holding thought by bio-chemical ion synchronization.

Psychic Suggestion - the insertion of a concept into the conscious mind for correcting inappropriate behavior and suggesting to choose the correct behavior for the situation. Psychic suggestion is merely a suggestion and does not possess the power to change conscious will only influence it.

Psycho Path - person who is out of touch with reality with cyclic desires to hurt people. New correct term is **Sociopath**. For example this Sociopath may have a strong desire to stab people with a knife every 90 days but this temporary desire is thwarted by police, friends, counselors, and the simple lack of an opportunity to do so.

Push - outward projection of thought or image from conscious mind to outside world.

Reality - truth, facts, sound reasoning, validated logic blocks.

Recognition - knowing what a concept is or assembling bits and pieces for the total image identification, giving rise to conscious notice or attention to image.

Reduction of Motion is the telepathic ability to slightly slow things down that already contains energy of motion through applying telepathy focus and synchronization.

Resonance with Telepathy - intensifying the volume of sounds through the synchronizing of sound resonance with telepathy. Unison of synchronized sound amplified with telepathy.

Saturation - density of color an image possesses.

Secondary Synchronization - the human brain uses bio-chemical energy to first synchronize a psychic thought that results in the thought's capture and containment in the conscious for ordinary thinking. For telepathy to occur in the beginning learning stages of telepathy the thought must be synchronized with a physical world auxiliary helper for a 2nd time to push the telepathic thought into the universal mind where all people will recognize and view the telepathic thought.

Short Term Memory - decays after 72 hours. Inputs into long term memory and dreams out through the pre-conscious when asleep.

Sign Language - a language expressed through hand and finger gestures for deaf people.

Simultaneous - occurring at exactly the same time.

Sociopath - person who is out of touch with reality with cyclic desires to hurt people. Old term is Psycho Path. For example this Sociopath may have a strong desire to stab people with a knife every 90 days but this temporary desire is thwarted by police, friends, counselors, and the simple lack of an opportunity to do so.

Spatial Area - the unlimited expanse of the multi-dimensional internal mind.

Sub Conscious - exchanged freely with the terms pre-conscious, pre-cognitive area, or subliminal zone.

Subliminal - inadequate energy thoughts that fail to produce perception or functioning just below the threshold energy level of conscious awareness. Beyond recognition as totally clear thought, remaining in pre-conscious zone when lacking sufficient energy to be noticed in the conscious.

Subliminal Zone - exchanged freely with the terms pre-conscious, pre-cognitive zone, or sub-conscious.

Summation Energy - adding psychic energy to a shared viewed concept by telepathy focus for clearer recognition in the conscious by two or more people in summation.

Summation in Neural Pathways - aggregation of impulse energy from a number of neural pathway systems synchronized and joined together by telepathy of which one system alone would not register a response. Summation telepathy psychic energy is used to overcome a damaged neural pathway or one its junction boxes and push the thought forward to the conscious again.

Summation Group - individuals in co-operation for the same goal using telepathy techniques for constructing and enhancing shared construction of such goals.

Summation Telepathy - more than one individual practicing mental telepathy providing for increased results and an increase in conscious perception by adding psychic energy and also pieces from both peoples' memories.

Synchronization - two or more things occurring at exactly the same time. To operate together simultaneously.

Telekinetics is the theory of putting things in motion. No one at this time can do Telekinetics.

Telepathy - Greek origin. **Tele=far and pathein=to experience or feel.** According to this definition the word mental has to be added for indication of the human mind but generally all the terms are interchangeable.

Telepathy Drift - Casual, unsynchronized telepathy communication without conscious effort.

Telepathy Summation Strengthening is when a person is ill, or mentally ill other people may use telepathy to align and strengthen his or her conscious threshold barrier that helps keep deviant and other trash thoughts out of the conscious focus.

Thought Transference - another name for telepathy or mind to mind exchange of ideas.

Threshold Energy Barrier - stimulus energy needed to cause a reaction or chain reaction to break a thought through this barrier into the conscious for recognition. If threshold energy is not enough then the response or concept is failed to be noticed by the conscious and thought remains in pre-conscious zone.

Threshold Barrier Wall - a wall between the pre-conscious and conscious allowing the conscious to concentrate on the current focused concept without interference from pre-conscious and its contents.

Transparency - with increased practice of telepathy the conscious mind automatically begins to be viewed by all people in close proximity, normally within 100 meters. In addition the most recent parts of the short term memory and a few pre-conscious high energy thoughts are able to be viewed by this phenomenon.

Truth - facts, sound reasoning, validation of concept.

Universal Mind - When practicing Flip all humans in the universe transmit to this single mind and receive from this same single mind of the universe. So there are an infinite number of physical brains existing in the universe but in reality only one mind in the universe that we as human physical brains interconnect to for telepathy. I give this dimension of telepathy the name Universal mind, also referred to in this book as the 3rd work place for summation. Telepathy concept transmissions take all aware conscious minds familiar and also those simply in close proximity into this universal mind dimension automatically by synchronization of a particular thought.

Universal Social Conscience - see World Social Conscience

Valid - well founded, effective techniques. Truth

Validation - confirm or substantiate, verification of communications. Rule out variables.

Vehicle - All thought is contained in fields of psychic energy. All these containers of psychic energy thought become the vehicle or transmission of mental telepathy thought.

Vividness is the illumination or brightness of image concept.

World Conscience is the world's common sense obligation to do good concerning what the vast majority of the world considers right. Ethical and emotional sensitive regards for people of the world. World Conscience exerts moral weight on an individual's mind by the total aggregate of human minds merged into a universal mind formed by mental telepathy to choose the most logical choice that normally is also the moral one. The World Conscience is a living working memory composed of all physical human brains moral memories found inside the universal mind.

INDEX

CPSIA information can be obtained at www.ICGtesting.com
Printed in the USA
LVOW05s1636090714

393593LV00008B/607/P